JOHN CAGE · MERCE CUNNINGHAM · JASPER JOHNS

Dancers on a Plane

CAGE · CUNNINGHAM · JOHNS

SUSAN SONTAG
In Memory of their Feelings

Richard Francis   Mark Rosenthal   Anne Seymour

David Sylvester   David Vaughan

Anthony d'Offay Gallery

1989

Cover: Jasper Johns *Dancers on a Plane* 1979
Oil on canvas with objects $77\frac{7}{8} \times 64$ inches
Collection of the artist

Frontispiece: John Cage, Jasper Johns and Merce Cunningham
Photograph by Timothy Greenfield-Sanders, July 1989

Anthony d'Offay Gallery, London
31 October to 2 December 1989

Tate Gallery, Liverpool
23 January to 25 March 1990

First published in 1989 by
Anthony d'Offay Gallery Dering Street London W1

ISBN 0 947564 29 2 hardbound
ISBN 0 947564 28 4 paperbound

© Anthony d'Offay Gallery, 1989

Designed by Simon Rendall and Anthony d'Offay
Edited by Judy Adam
Printed by Dr. Cantz'sche Druckerei, Stuttgart, West Germany

Foreword

9

SUSAN SONTAG
In Memory of their Feelings

13

Introduction by Richard Francis

25

JOHN CAGE
Solo for Piano from
Concert for Piano and Orchestra 1957-58

36

Points in Space by David Sylvester

47

MERCE CUNNINGHAM
Photographs 1940-1981

57

Merce Cunningham by David Vaughan

81

JASPER JOHNS
Paintings and Drawings 1979-1982

92

Dancers on a Plane and other Stratagems
for Inclusion in the Work of Jasper Johns
by Mark Rosenthal

115

Works in the Exhibition

136

Chronologies

147

Acknowledgements

165

Mystical form of Samvara with seventy-four arms embracing his sakti with twelve arms.
Painting, Nepal, 17th century. Mookerjee Collection.

FOREWORD

'"In this very body", Buddha said, "six feet in length, with its sense impression and its thoughts and ideas, are the world, the origin of the world, the ceasing of the world and likewise the way that leads to the ceasing thereof". If we can analyse one human being, we shall have analysed the whole universe, because it is built on the same plane.'

Ajit Mookerjee, *Tantra Art*, 1971

This book was made to accompany an exhibition of the work of three friends, who between them have extended the frontiers of the arts for much of the century and at approximately sixty, seventy and eighty, show no signs of abandoning their positions. They are also notable for disallowing the presence of boundaries within their own disciplines and for moving in and out of each other's domains in the best traditions of friendship, each respecting the autonomy of each.

John Cage, composer and catalyst extraordinary, was born in 1912, the year Marcel Duchamp painted *Nude Descending a Staircase* and began work on *The Large Glass*. In 1938 Cage met Merce Cunningham in Seattle, at Bonnie Bird's dance class at the Cornish Academy, where he had taken a job as accompanist-composer. Cage had completed his studies with Schönberg in Los Angeles and was developing his interest in percussion and the use of ambient sound to make music. His first work for prepared piano was created the same year. Merce Cunningham (born in 1919) was only eighteen, at the beginning of his studies in modern dance, yet to become a choreographer, but already exhibiting an unusual appreciation of the arts as a whole. His first collaboration with John Cage, *Credo in Us* (choreographed with Jean Erdman) dates from 1942. Jasper Johns (born in 1930) met both Cage and Cunningham in 1954, the year he made *Construction with Toy Piano* (reproduced p.118) and started his first Flag painting. His initial involvement with the Cunningham Dance Company was through helping his friend

9

Robert Rauschenberg, who in 1954 began a long connection with the Company as Artistic Adviser. In 1958 with Rauschenberg and Emile de Antonio, Johns was one of the organizers of the John Cage Retrospective Concert at New York Town Hall. This was also the occasion of the first performance, conducted by Merce Cunningham, of the *Concert for Piano and Orchestra*, the piano part of which is exhibited in the present exhibition. In 1960 the same friends organized a similar event for Merce Cunningham at the Phoenix Theater, New York. Jasper Johns did his first designs for the Cunningham Company in 1961 and became its Artistic Adviser in 1967.

From the point of view of this exhibition such collaborative activities offer, however, a pretext and a structure rather than a primary subject of focus. The purpose of the undertaking is neither to present the details of a relationship, nor is it to define the connections between art, music and dance on a documentary level. In any case the patterns and intensities of friendship change according to external pressures on the individuals involved. It seemed more profoundly interesting to explore how the three disciplines interact, to focus on common themes and preoccupations and to take the opportunity to consider the individual arts as contributing to a larger whole, a single unity.

The key to the exhibition is to be found in *Dancers on a Plane*, the title given by Jasper Johns to three of his pictures painted between 1979 and 1981. The two largest form a pair. The third is essentially a smaller version of the second. In Tantra the individual being and the universal being are one, and everything that exists in the universe exists in the human body. Johns based the *Dancers on a Plane* pictures on a Tantric painting depicting Samvara (a Buddhist deity reflecting forms of the god Siva) in ecstatic union with his sakti. This scene represents metaphorically the reconciliation through enlightenment of the opposing forces of creation and destruction. Siva has many faces, one of which is Lord of the Dance; in an earlier age *Dancers on a Plane* would probably have been called 'Portrait of Merce Cunningham as the Lord Siva'.

Johns's choice of metaphor seems not only to indicate the parallels in his work with Cunningham's but to reflect the impulse beneath the work of the twentieth century avant-garde in general to create as nature creates rather than to imitate her outward appearance. It expresses the direct way in which these three artists work with the space, time and substance of the world around them, energetic or quiet, visible or invisible, audible or inaudible. Whether, as in the case of John Cage, they do so with ambient sound, or like Cunningham with use of the energies of the body or like Johns with ideas, sense impressions and perceptions expressed in visual terms.

We asked David Sylvester to write about John Cage, David Vaughan to write about Merce Cunningham and Mark Rosenthal to write about Jasper Johns and we are much indebted to their insights. We are also grateful to Richard Francis who has written the Introduction. The main text to the book is by Susan Sontag with the idea that it should be more part of the exhibition than about it. Her writing is as autonomous as the contributions by the exhibitors. In four dimensions our concept of this relationship has grown correspondingly more profound. We are indeed grateful for her collaboration.

The artists have made an enormous contribution to making this exhibition work and we cannot thank them enough. All of them have given unstintingly of their time and energy. They have lent pictures, answered questions, corrected chronologies and borne the brunt of visits. Their friends and assistants have been pressed into service – we are especially grateful to Sarah Taggart and David Vaughan. The exhibition could not have taken place without the help and encouragement of Bill Katz. We would also like to thank Timothy Greenfield-Sanders for his portrait photographs of the artists taken together this year. Last but not least we must acknowledge the generosity of the lenders to the exhibition, who have responded so enthusiastically to the idea we have put to them: The Art Institute of Chicago; Robert and Jane Meyerhoff; Northwestern University Music Library, Evanston; The Trustees of the Tate Gallery and the private collectors who wish to remain anonymous. We thank them all.

AS and Ad'O

In Memory of their Feelings

1. DANCERS ON A PLANE

I don't see them.

There. The dancers are there, invisible – an analogue to racing thoughts.

Framed by the utensils of eating.

A meal to be eaten?

An invisible meal.

Two meals: one light, one dark. One sprightly, one stained with sexual dread.

Dancers on a plate?

No. They need more space than that.

2. EATING AND DANCING

Recombinant arts.

A domain of pleasure. A domain of courtesy.

Rule-bound. Who sets the rules? Behaviour with standards.

An idea of order. First one thing, then another. Then one is full. Then it is finished – the belly sated, the limbs heavy. After a decent interval: then again. All over again. All over, again.

They remind us we live in the body-house.

Living 'in' the body. But where else could we live?

Dancing as the realm of freedom, that's less than half the story.

Eating as the realm of necessity. Not necessarily. What about eating idyllically (as in Paris)?

Everyone eats, everyone can dance. Not every one dances (alas).

I watch dance, with pleasure. I don't watch eating. If I watch someone eating when hungry, I wish it were I eating. A meal watched by a hungry person is always savoury. If I watch someone eating when full, I may turn away.

You can dance for me. (You do the dancing in my place, I'll just watch.) You can't eat for me. Not much pleasure there . . . .

You can dance to please : Salome. You can eat to please, too : as a child might eat to please its mother or a nurse. (As Suzanne Farrell is said to have said that she danced for God and for Mr Balanchine.) But except to doting parents eating is a poor spectator sport. Mildly disgusting unless you're doing it as well.

To eat is to put metal in one's mouth. Delicately. It's not supposed to hurt.

The eater fills the hole.

A dancer eats space.

Space eats time.

Sounds eat silence.

3. THE KNIFE

It cuts. Don't be afraid. This is not a weapon. It's just a tool to help you eat. See. Passing it to you – you asked for it – I proffer it by the handle, keeping the blade pointed at myself. The blade is pointing at me.

One should not move the point of the knife toward someone as in an attack.

You can lay it down two ways. Blade in, blade out.

14

Don't be timorous. It isn't sharp. It's just a plain, ordinary . . . knife. Straight. Two-sided.

In the fairy tale, a mermaid who has fallen in love with a prince begs to be allowed to assume human form so she can leave the water and make her way to the court. Yes. She will have legs, she will walk. But with each step she takes it will feel as if she were walking on knives.

You can dance with a knife. (Between the teeth? Between the shoulder blades?) Hard to imagine dancing with a fork. Or with a spoon.

The knife seems like the master utensil, the one from which all others depend. (Swiss Army Knife.) You could spear food with your knife, eliminating the fork. (As everyone knows, you *can* eat the peas with your knife. You're just not supposed to.) As for the spoon – well, we could do without that, too. Just lift up the bowl dish cup, and drink it.

Only the knife is really necessary. And it is the knife, more than any other eating utensil, whose use is most restricted. The evolution of table manners is mainly about what to do with knives. Use the knife more and more unobtrusively, elegantly. With your fingerends. Don't grasp it against your palm, like a stick.

'There is a tendency that slowly permeates civilized society, from the top to the bottom, to restrict the use of the knife (within the framework of existing eating techniques) and wherever possible not to use the instrument at all' (Norbert Elias). For instance, to eliminate or at least limit the contact of the knife with round or egg-shaped objects. Not all restrictions are successful. The prohibition on eating fish with a knife, once fairly strict, was circumvented by the introduction of a special fish knife.

That oxymoron : the butter knife.

To eat is to put metal in one's mouth. But not knives. The mere sight of someone putting her knife in her mouth produces an uneasy feeling.

4. THE SPOON

The spoon seems to belong in the mouth.

The spoon is not quite grown-up in the way the knife and fork are. It doesn't menace. It isn't a tamed weapon.

The spoon is the utensil of childhood, the friendliest utensil. The spoon is a child – or child-like – forever. Yum yum. Scoop me up, pour me in. Like a cradle, a shovel, a hand cupped. Doesn't cut or pierce or impale. It accepts. Round, curved. Can't stick you. Don't trust your child with a knife or a fork, but how can a spoon harm? The spoon is itself a child.

The world is full of pleasures. One has only to be where one is. Here. Now.

Give me my spoon, my big spoon, and I'll eat the world. A metal spoon is an afterthought. While a wooden knife is less of a knife, a wooden spoon isn't less of a spoon. It's just fine.

'Spooning' : embracing, kissing, petting. Lovers in bed fit together, in sleep, like spoons.

To bring about a music 'that will be part of the noises of the environment, will take them into consideration. I think of it as melodious, softening the noises of the knives and forks, not dominating them, not imposing itself', wrote John Cage, quoting Erik Satie.

What happened to the spoons? Don't spoons make noises, too?

Softer noises.

And music. Music is made with two spoons (not with two forks, two knives).

Spoon music.

5. THE FORK

There's a hesitation about the fork. You hold down the food with the fork in your left hand while you cut it with the knife held in your right. Then – if you're not only right handed but also American – you put down the knife, then transfer the fork to your right hand and send the speared morsel up to your mouth.

Grown-ups throw knives. Children throw spoons. Nobody (I think) would throw a fork. It may be four-thirds of a toy trident, but it can't be thrown as one. It wouldn't arrive, spear-like, tines first.

The weight is in the handle.

The fork as emblem – emblem of the real. Jasper Johns, explaining something about 'my general development so far', said: 'That is to say, I find it more interesting to use a real fork as a painting than it is to use painting as a real fork.'

What would a fork that wasn't real look like?

The fork is the youngest of the three great eating utensils. The Last Supper was set with knives and spoons only. No forks either at the wedding feast in Cana.

It made its appearance when the knife and spoon were well established. Invented in Italy, thought a foppish pretension when it arrived in England in the early 17th century: a set of gold 'Italian forkes' presented to Elizabeth I by the Venetian ambassador were put on display at Westminster; she never used them.

The principle of fastidiousness. Embodied in objects that now could hardly seem more everyday, plain . . . .

The introduction of that vital implement, the fork (for a long time despised as effete), enabled people to distance themselves from the eating process by avoiding manual contact with the food.

New forms of distance, new forms of delicacy.

New rules of finicky behaviour at table proliferated. People were expected to manipulate an increasingly complicated battery of utensils.

It seemed hard, setting up and keeping this distance.

Now we take forks for granted.

6. KNIFE, SPOON, FORK

A secular trinity – knife, spoon, fork.

No hierarchy. The list can only be varied, systematically. As in knife, fork, spoon. As in fork, knife, spoon. As in fork, spoon, knife. As in spoon, fork, knife. As in spoon, knife, fork.

Seemingly immutable (after all that history).

They lie there, flat. On a plain (plane) surface. Perpendicular to the edge of the table.

A trialogue.

A stately relationship. Not all on the same side of the plate. Three divides into two and one. Fork on the left side. Knife and spoon on the right.

The knife is scary by itself. But as part of a setting, something else. Lying beside the spoon, the knife becomes quite . . . domestic. Knife and spoon : the odd couple.

They don't go together, you don't use them together. But they *are* together.

The fork is solitary. Always is. Even in an ampler setting, all you could have next to it is another (smaller, larger) fork.

That's how they're arranged at the start of the meal, one step down from the plate. Escorting the plate on either side.

No excuse now to eat with your hands. Civil eating (versus gluttony).

After finishing eating you arrange them neatly on the plate.

Not alphabetically. Not in order of importance, if there were one.

A trinity but quite contingent.

They seem to complement each other.

We have learned to use all three. But they can be taken separately, of course.

7. DANCERS ON A PLAIN

On a plane? An airplane?

On a plain. As open (borderless) as feasible.

Low, level. Don't try for any of those old heights. Depths.

What is essential about a surface that makes it different from another surface? How do we experience smoothness in a surface, a movement, a sound, an experience?

Smoothness?

Yes. Something continues, plausibly.

Pleasurably. With parts.

What does it mean to say of something that it is one part of something (a surface, a movement, a sound, an experience)?

The old heights. Mirroring. Look down. These are my genitals.

Be more modest. (Elegant.)

Sometimes light, sometimes heavy – it's all right to be heavy sometimes.

Make it new. Yes. And make it plain.

8. SYMMETRIES

Dancers on a plane. No centre. Always off-side. Any place is the centre.

We seem symmetrical. Two eyes, two ears, two arms, two legs; two ovaries
– or two hairy testicles. But we're not. Something is always dominating.

A mirror image : a fantasy of symmetry. The right the reverse of the left, or
vice versa.

We *seem* symmetrical. But we are not.

They cross-refer (knife, spoon, fork). As in the brain. Right-handedness means
the left side of the brain is dominant. Left-handedness means the brain's right
side dominates.

How to find out which side of your brain is dominant. Close your eyes, think of a
question, then slowly think of an answer to the question. If while you're doing
this you turn your head slightly to the right, that means the left side dominates.

And vice versa.

The question-master.

An art that asks questions.

How do we understand how one part of a surface, a movement, a sound, an
experience relates to another? Note : you have a choice of questions. But if *that's*
the question you choose to ask, you can be sure the answer will include a bias
toward asymmetry.

'The non-relationship of the movement,' Cunningham has declared, 'is extended into a relationship with music. It is essentially a non-relationship.'

The dancer must be light. Food makes you heavy.

You eat with your hands, dance on your legs. Eating can be right-handed or left-handed. Is dancing left-legged or right-legged?

Any place is the centre.

A real symmetry: chopsticks.

9. SILENCES

Lots of prattle. That, too, is a kind of silence. (Since there is no silence.) The deaf hear their deafness. The blind see their blindness.

Controlling through silence. Whoever speaks less is the stronger.

Is there a warm silence?

The noise of ideas.

Take it to language.

No, take it to babble. Cut up the words in strips, like raw vegetables. Make meals out of words. A culinary relation to words . . . .

Suppose Knife, Spoon, and Fork are three people. And they get together on a plane (plain). What would they have to say to each other?

I know. 'Who brought the marshmallows?'

Mushrooms, surely you mean mushrooms.

As I said, marshmallows.

That's not what I had in mind. Then what?

Then they get very particular about how the marshmallows are to be cooked.

All three of them know a lot about food. (About eating. Preceded by gathering, preparing, cooking . . . .)

But these are just marshmallows. American junk.

You can be fastidious about anything. And marshmallows can be botched, too; can disappoint. It's a question of (yes, once again) the relation of inside to outside. The inside has to be cooked very well, while not letting the outside catch fire. Ideally the outside will get crusty but not burnt, while the inside melts. Then, right before it falls off the stick, you pluck it off with your fingers and pop it whole into your mouth.

Stick? What happened to the fork? Don't you toast marshmallows with a fork?

All right, the fork. But this is better as a gooey experience than as a refined one.

'Everywhere and at all times,' Lévi-Strauss has observed, 'the European code of politeness rules out the possibility of eating noisily.'

And you don't always have to be polite.

10. IN MEMORY OF OUR FEELINGS

In the first — buoyant, allegro vivace — painting, this is real flatware that has been painted white. In the second, heavy painting, the artist has cast the utensils in bronze.

Repeating as a means of varying. Accepting as a way of discriminating. Indifference as a form of emotional vitality.

Use me as you will.

Savouring non-relatedness. Put the emphasis on savouring. 'I am more interested in the *facts* of moving rather than in my feelings about them' (Merce Cunningham).

Would you like to play chess? Chess seriously.

We were younger then. Who would have thought then – when we were younger; then – that it would be like this?

We meet. This could be at a dinner party (forks, knives, spoons, etc.)

We say things like, How lovely to see you. I've been busy. I think so. I don't know. That must have been very interesting. (Everything is interesting. But some things are more interesting than others.) Probably not. I've heard. In Frankfurt, in Illinois, in London. Next year. What a pity. He's gone away. He'll be back soon. They're organizing something. You'll get an invitation.

We smile. We nod. We are indefatigable. I think I'm free next week. We say we wish we saw more of each other.

We eat, we savour.

Meanwhile, each harbours a secret idea of ascending, of descending. We go on. The plane's edge beckons.

Susan Sontag

'If Art is not Art, then what is it?'[1]

'Why do you always ask about the relationship or connections between us? Let me put it to you this way. Don't you see that the fan is here and that the Norfolk Pine is there? How in Heaven's name are they related? If you can answer that then you can answer these other questions . . .

Well, they are in the same space and the same time and they're not interfering with one another. In Zen this is called non-obstruction. But they interpenetrate; I can look at both at the same time and in me they become an experience which may not be the same as comes to someone else . . . It's quite an amusing thing to look at those two things and put them together. And you can't say what their relationship is except by saying they are both here together.

There is no intention . . . nor any intention when [a] dance is made.'[2]

Jasper Johns has made three paintings with the title *Dancers on a Plane* inscribed in stencil lettering running from left to right at the base, beginning on the central axis; interspersed between the letters is, in one of the paintings, the artist's name and in the other two Merce Cunningham's name. These names run from right to left. Johns made the large, predominantly white painting first – he describes it as having a 'Stable, rigid, heroic mood' a 'sense of balance between left and right' connected with the symmetry of the human body'[3] and says its subject is thus in some ways concerned with the idea of dance mediated through the formal language of painting. The dancer that he was thinking about is drawn from Tantric images of Siva. He said recently that the images referred to are 'creation and destruction . . . mating . . . life and death and such. All a kind of dancing. Dance must have its roots in that same kind of expressiveness, I should think.'[4]

There are many images of Siva as Lord of the Dance, but the particular one which inspired Johns was a Tantric painting from Nepal, which he had seen reproduced in

Ajit Mookerjee's book on Tantra, showing Siva copulating with Sakti. The gods are on the central axis of the paintings, where the dancer and the *lingam* or erect penis is usually depicted. The subject, we can assume, is both mortality and sexuality and this appears again most obviously in the *Tantric Detail* paintings where the *lingam* is made literal by the depiction of the penis and testicles. Johns obviously does not describe the dancer in paint but here, as Rosenthal suggests, is the presence of a dancing figure within the interstices of the crosshatched image.

Johns talks of the figure of the dancer on the picture plane and appearing to penetrate it and stand in front of it. The act of dancing creates the ambiguity of the picture surface, something which he further emphasizes through the crosshatching technique. The picture plane becomes the arena for the events of the dancer's activity. The central axis of the painting also divides the picture into an image and its mirror which in the first painting is repeated almost faithfully creating the equable image of stability. In the Tate's painting the image is disturbed and unbalanced, 'thrown into [a] display of unequal energy'. This is partly a result of the disruption of the crosshatched pattern and partly the aggressive modification of the palette. These paintings become a meditation on the painted image and the presence of the dancing figure in relation to the physical restraints of the depiction system.

Johns has always used images from the everyday world, often they are things to which he has ascribed particular personal significance as representatives of the emotional. The drawing *Perilous Night* (pl.14) brings together several such images. On the left is part of an enlargement from Grünewald's Isenheim altarpiece with a detail of the Resurrection's fallen soldier turned through ninety degrees. The righthand side of the drawing shows an arm, probably imprinted by Johns himself, as in earlier works, and the cover and score of the John Cage composition *The Perilous Night*, a work for prepared piano first published in 1943-44. John Cage has referred to the 'perilous night' as a particularly dark period in his own life. He says that the image came from an Irish folk tale which he remembers in a collection made by Joseph Campbell. For him, the music tells a story of the dangers of the erotic life and describes the misery of 'something that was together that is split apart'.

This combination of attention to the everyday, and a profound meditation on the mystery of it, offers almost certainly the richest source of connection between the work of all three artists. None of them is intentionally inelegant but they all use the ordinary as the source of the art that they create. The artists work together in public only when they contribute to dance performances of the Cunningham Company. The performances are unlike those of classical ballet since the three components of movement, sound and design are connected not by the story of the dance but confront the fragmented and non-linear experience of the modern world. Their allegiance to the modern experience is apparent, and the complexity of that experience, its potential to alienate or isolate the individual, is offered in uncompromisingly modern terms.

Born in Los Angeles in 1912, John Cage is the oldest of the three; his contribution, especially his thinking and writing, is acknowledged by several generations of artists. Jasper Johns says of him that he is 'Part preacher, part teacher . . . always filled with ideas and curious about ideas.' Cage teaches in the manner of a Zen master – by not teaching – and denies that his influence has been intentional. The introduction of techniques derived from Eastern methods to his own practice has affected dance, music and the visual arts. The use of Buddhist and Tantric ideas, specifically in respect of non-intervention and contingency, runs through the work of the three artists. Cage's espousal of Zen and chance and the inevitable consequences of chance operations, was both highly seductive and a revelatory escape for many artists. Morton Feldman, the composer and writer said '. . . John changed everything. We got out of that straitjacket, and it made everything much more simple in one way and a lot harder in other ways. What we learned was *there are no catastrophes.*'[5]

Cage met Merce Cunningham at a dance class in Seattle in 1938, where he had been invited by the teacher Bonnie Bird to be the accompanist. Cunningham, born in 1919, had come to Seattle from Centralia, a small town in Washington State to study Drama and Dance at the Cornish School. He studied for two years before moving to New York where he became a soloist in the Martha Graham Dance Company. Cunningham was dissatisfied with the emotional and narrative content of Graham's dance and was looking for a new way of working which would present movement itself. He began to choreograph solos for himself, for which he devised a new technique that added elements of classical ballet and of the Graham-based modern dance to his own ideas. Cage composed music to be presented simultaneously with the dance and while, at the beginning, the dance and music were closely related through their common use of the same rhythmic structure, over the next two decades they became linked only by being presented in the same space at the same time.

Cage and Cunningham worked together from 1942 and Cunningham eventually formed his own dance company. They were invited to the experimental Black Mountain College summer school in North Carolina in 1948 and again in 1952 and 1953; they had very little money and used this as an opportunity to work as a group over several weeks each year. Prominent among the artists at Black Mountain was Robert Rauschenberg, who by 1952 had become virtually artist in residence and a key member of the group each summer. Rauschenberg acknowledged that Cage's ideas allowed him to develop his own ideas about the everyday in the work of art; the influence was mutual since Cage has said that the white paintings of 1952 that he saw at Black Mountain gave him the courage to present his 'silent' piece, 4'33" for piano in the same year. In 1954 Rauschenberg became Artistic Adviser to the Dance Company.

Jasper Johns, born in 1930 in Augusta, Georgia and educated briefly in South Carolina and New York, met Rauschenberg and Cage in 1954. Johns was painting and supporting himself by working in a bookshop. He moved to a building on Pearl Street and soon after Rauschenberg moved into the loft below. They worked together as freelance display artists and, in 1954, Rauschenberg was invited to be the designer for *Minutiae* by Cunningham presented in Brooklyn with *Music for Piano* by Cage. Johns assisted Rauschenberg on sets and costumes for the Cunningham Dance Company during the period that Rauschenberg was Artistic Adviser (1954-1964). There are many stories about the way in which Rauschenberg and Johns improvised, often at the last minute, to solve the inevitable practical problems of staging new dances. In 1967 Johns succeeded Rauschenberg as the Artistic Adviser to the Company and invited artists such as Warhol, Stella, Nauman, Morris and Jenney to make contributions to specific dances. Johns is reported by Cage and Cunningham to dislike the uncontrolled aspects of the theatre and he characteristically avoids conflict: '[The] idea of making something that would distract from the dance never interested me and I never had any thought of enrichment – that I could make the thing more complex. I just tried to do something that would not interfere with what was happening . . . This was probably to do with manners . . . to try to get the work done but not to appear in it.'[6]

Cunningham has written of the desire to approach everyday experience in dance; his interest is in the confusion of a crowded street as much as an aesthetic dance movement. 'I was looking out the window one morning and there were several children out there. They were skipping and running about playing, little kids, and I suddenly realised they were dancing, you could call it dancing, and yet it wasn't dancing; I thought it was marvellous. There was no music.'[7] Cunningham makes the dance on his own in a studio where he establishes the routines and decides the order and dancers. It is at this moment that he does his 'paperwork' (what Cage calls composition) – the notes of times and sequences that become the basis for the choreography. He works with the dancers to put the dance on them during an intense period (of up to four weeks) prior to the first performance. Cage and Cunningham often do not discuss the music that will be played with the dance before the performance. Occasionally they will have a brief conversation of a practical nature before the event. However when the music has been ascribed to a dance it remains with it and is used for subsequent performances. On some occasions the music has been written separately from the dance and used because it works. *Second Hand*, for example, has a complex but exemplary history; it began as a Cunningham solo to the first movement of Erik Satie's *Socrate* and Cage urged Cunningham to complete the *Socrate*. Nearly ten years later, Cunningham made a duet and company dance for the second and third movements. Cage finished the two piano arrangements but the French publisher refused permission for its use. 'So what John did was to write a new piece using the same phraseology, the same rhythm, changing the melody of the *Socrate* by means of chance operations . . . John said he was going to call his piece *Cheap Imitation* so that the title, not just the music, would imitate Satie.'[8] The dance was called *Second Hand* in response to the music's title.

The manuscript shown in this exhibition, the *Solo for Piano* from the *Concert for Piano and Orchestra*, was used for *Antic Meet* a dance for which Robert Rauschenberg made the costumes, objects and lighting designs. It was used, Cage says, because it was just completed and because the solo piano part had been written for David Tudor, a fine and accurate performer of Cage's music (who since then has become one of the principal composers with the Company). It was also used because it was easily transported without the great cost of paying for an orchestra (though whenever possible an orchestra was used) and perhaps because it marked a crucially important stage in the development of Cage's music. *The Concert for Piano and Orchestra* was premiered at the concert arranged as a twenty-five year retrospective by his friends at Town Hall in New York in May 1958. Robert Rauschenberg, Jasper Johns and Emile de Antonio joined forces to produce the concert, David Tudor selected the music and Merce Cunningham agreed to be the conductor. The concert was to include the new work which Cage was freed to complete. Cage's music not only used chance but employed it as a discipline requiring the invention of many new compositional notations, partly in deference, he says, to the abundant variety of nature. Cage spent several weeks working day and night to complete the manuscript which appears unlike any previous conventionally written music. Since the music is defined by time rather than movements or bars guided by the conductor, Cunningham's role was to act as a human chronometer. Cage said 'The only thing I was being consistent to in this piece was that I did not need to be consistent.'

In 1968 the Company presented the dance *Walkaround Time* for which Johns made the set based on Marcel Duchamp's *The Large Glass* (*The Bride stripped bare by her Bachelors, even*). It seems that the idea for the dance came from a conversation that Johns and Cunningham had at an evening at Duchamp's house. Johns suggested to Cunningham that a dance could be constructed using the images of parts of Duchamp's seminal work disposed in various ways around the stage. Cunningham agreed and Johns immediately went over to Duchamp and asked if he would also agree to it. Duchamp asked 'But who would do all the work?' Johns replied that he would; relieved, Duchamp gave permission. He only asked that at some point in the dance the work should be seen with its parts related in the same way as the original work. Johns supervised the manufacture of the pieces, changing the dimensions to make them capable of being free-standing and moveable. When the elements were shipped to Buffalo for the first performance it was found that the stage was smaller than anticipated and Cunningham modified the dance to accommodate the new scale. Cunningham himself has said that there are several further references to Duchamp and his work in the piece. For example, David Vaughan suggests that the opening sequence, which is taken from the exercises with which Cunningham begins his daily class, can be considered 'readymades'.

Cage claims that he has freed his work from expressiveness, taken from it the artist's intentions, created in the arena a 'purposeful purposelessness'. The effect of the work becomes its most significant characteristic since it exists fully only when the audience receives it. Cage explains it as follows: 'Things become more useful expressively when they are not expressed by the artist but (when they are expressed by the person) receiving them. How better can that be expressed except in the audience?'⁹ Cunningham has echoed this repeatedly, saying of his dance and its audiences. 'Between the two they can produce something else, something, say I, myself, wouldn't have thought.'¹⁰ As Cage put it, 'not self expression but self alteration'. It allows the audience to concentrate on the experience which they, as receivers, find in each of the art forms and liberates the artists to work in a necessary way with their media. Thus Cage can claim *only* to be making sounds vibrate, and that his writing though it comes from ideas, is not about them but unintentionally produces them, that Cunningham's work is not about dancing but *is* the dance. Our role, in front of Johns's paintings, as receivers, and makers for ourselves, of the experience, is not different from that of being a participant in the audience of a theatre or concert hall. The paintings demand from us our own activity of looking.

Cage's recent lectures given as the Charles Eliot Norton Lectures at Harvard have surprised that institution since they were not informative, but were performances, the reading of his non-syntactic mesostics. He ends the introductory note to the series in a way that characterizes almost all of his work. 'In the nature of the use of chance operations is the belief that all answers answer all questions. The non-homogeneity that characterizes the source material of these lectures suggests that anything says what you have to say, that meaning is in the breath, that without thinking we can tell what is being said without understanding it.'[11]

Richard Francis

1   John Cage in conversation with the author, New York, 27 June 1989
2   *Ibid.*
3   Jasper Johns in conversation with the author, New York, 27 June 1989
4   *Ibid.*
5   Quoted in Calvin Tomkins, *Ahead of the Game* (Harmondsworth, 1968), p.106
6   Jasper Johns in conversation with the author, New York, 27 June 1989
7   Jacqueline Lesschaeve, *The Dancer and the Dance* (New York and London, 1985), p.73
8   Lesschaeve, op cit., p.88
9   John Cage in conversation with the author, New York, 27 June 1989
10 From an interview with Jeremy Isaacs broadcast on BBC Television, The Late Show, 5 April 1989
11 Unpublished lecture notes for the introduction to the Charles Eliot Norton Lectures, given at Harvard University, Cambridge, Massachusetts, 1988

JOHN CAGE

Born Los Angeles, California 1912

CONCERT FOR PIANO AND ORCHESTRA
SOLO FOR PIANO

FOR ELAINE DE KOONING

STONY POINT, N.Y., J.C.1957-8

Solo for Piano, Concert for Piano and Orchestra 1957-58, 11 × 16⅞ inches

PIANO

EACH PAGE IS ONE SYSTEM FOR A SINGLE PIANIST TO BE PLAYED WITH OR WITHOUT ANY OR ALL PARTS WRITTEN FOR ORCHESTRAL INSTRUMENTS. THE WHOLE IS TO BE TAKEN AS A BODY OF MATERIAL PRESENTABLE AT ANY POINT BETWEEN MINIMUM (NOTHING PLAYED) AND MAXIMUM (EVERYTHING PLAYED), BOTH HORIZONTALLY AND VERTICALLY: A PROGRAM MADE WITHIN A DETERMINED LENGTH OF TIME (TO BE ALTERED BY A CONDUCTOR WHEN THERE IS ONE) MAY INVOLVE ANY READING, I.E., ANY SEQUENCE OF PARTS OR PARTS THEREOF.

A FOLLOWING THE PERIMETER, FROM ANY NOTE ON IT, PLAY IN OPPOSITE DIRECTIONS IN THE PROPORTION GIVEN. HERE AND ELSEWHERE, THE ABSENCE OF INDICATIONS OF ANY KIND MEANS FREEDOM FOR THE PERFORMER IN THAT REGARD.

B AN AGGREGATE MUST BE PLAYED AS A SINGLE ICTUS. WHERE THIS IS IMPOSSIBLE, THE UNPLAYABLE NOTES SHALL BE TAKEN AS HARMONICS PREPARED IN ADVANCE. HARMONICS MAY ALSO BE PRODUCED WHERE THEY ARE NOT SO REQUIRED. RESONANCES, BOTH OF AGGREGATES AND INDIVIDUAL NOTES OF THEM, MAY BE FREE IN LENGTH. OVERLAPPINGS, INTERPENETRATIONS, ARE ALSO FREE. THE SINGLE STAFF IS PROVIDED WITH 2 CLEF SIGNS. WHERE THESE DIFFER, AMBIGUITY OBTAINS IN THE PROPORTION INDICATED BY THE 2 NUMBERS ABOVE THE AGGREGATE, THE FIRST OF THESE APPLYING TO THE CLEF SIGN ABOVE THE STAFF. AN INKED IN RECTANGLE ABOVE A PAIR OF NOTES INDICATES A CHROMATIC CLUSTER.

C M = MUTE. P = PIZZ. ALL SINGLE TONES.

D LIKE B, BUT WITH VERTICAL ARPEGGIATION AND TIME TENDENCIES MAKING USE OF HARMONICS UNNECESSARY. THE ARPEGGIATION IS INDICATED BY DOUBLE ARROWS ACCOMPANIED BY A SERIES OF NUMBERS. THE SIGN ↕ 1,1,1 MEANS 1 NOTE IN THE MIDDLE FOLLOWED BY 1 NOTE HIGHER, OR LOWER, FOLLOWED BY 1 NOTE LOWER IF THE 2ND WAS HIGHER, HIGHER IF THE SECOND WAS LOWER. ↓ 2,1 MEANS TWO NOTES OF WHICH AT LEAST 1 IS THE HIGHEST OF THE THREE FOLLOWED BY A THIRD LOWER NOTE. THE HORIZONTAL ARROWS REFER TO TIME AND THE TENDENCY OF THE TONES TO SOUND SOONER, LATER, OR AT THE POINT OF NOTATION.

E PLAY WITH HANDS INDICATED. WHERE CLEFS DIFFER, A NOTE IS EITHER BASS OR TREBLE. THE NOTES HAVING A SINGLE STEM ARE TO BE ARPEGGIATED (UP OR DOWN). PLAY NOTATIONS FROM LEFT TO RIGHT.

F NUMBERS ARE SECONDS OR OTHER TIME UNITS.

G OF NOTES WRITTEN PLAY NUMBER GIVEN IN ANY MANNER (KEYS, HARP) BEGINNING AND ENDING AS INDICATED BY ARROW. DYNAMIC INDICATIONS ACCOMPANY EACH CIRCLE ON THE CIRCUMFERENCE OF WHICH THE NOTES ARE PLACED. (SCALE ppp - fff)

H ANY ONE OF THESE, AS IN C, OR ANY NUMBER (INCLUDING ALL) IN SEQUENCE, MAINTAINING, IN THE LATTER CASE, THE CLEF SIGN OF THE ONE FIRST PLAYED.

I PIZZ. WHERE INDICATED. A SINGLE TONE, INTERVAL, OR A 3 NOTE AGGREGATE. REAPPEARANCES OF TONES TO BE PLAYED AS ORIGINALLY.

J NUMBERS ARE OF NOTES TO BE PLAYED BETWEEN LIMITS CONNECTED BY LINES. ARROWS INDICATE DIRECTION IN SPACE-TIME BACKWARDS AND FORWARDS. A STRAIGHT LINE ABOVE A NUMBER MEANS ASCENDING OR DESCENDING GAMUT. ∿ MEANS ASCENDING AND DESCENDING.

K DISREGARD TIME. PLAY ONLY ODD OR EVEN NUMBER OF TONES IN A PERFORMANCE, USING OTHERS OF A GIVEN 3, 4, 5 OR 6 SIDED FIGURE AS GRACES OR PUNCTUATIONS.

L PLAY FROM LEFT TO RIGHT WITH HANDS INDICATED. CLEF AMBIGUITY AS IN B. PERIMETERS WERE COMPOSING MEANS AND DO NOT HERE AFFECT TIME, AS THEY DO IN A.

M BEGIN AT LEFT, END AT RIGHT, CHANGING DIRECTION AT INTERSECTIONS IF DESIRED. MAY BE EXPRESSED AS ONE VOICE, A 'COUNTERPOINT', OR AS 3 OR 4 VOICES. PEDALS ONLY IN AREAS INDICATED, NOT OBLIGATORY. ⌴ PED. L....I U.C. L. _ _⌋ SOSTENUTO.

N LIKE I, BUT WITH VARYING DYNAMICS. SOSTENUTO PEDAL GIVEN.

O AUDIBLE (AS CHORDS, LINES, ARPEGGIATIONS AS IN D BUT FREE, ETC.) ONLY BETWEEN HORIZONTAL LINES. PEDALS AS IN M.

P ANY NOISES (INCLUDING AUXILIARY), DYNAMICS OF WHICH ARE NOTATED.

Q LIKE M, BUT IN TIME (ANY UNITS); GOING BACK INCURS NEED FOR INCREASED SPEED.

R RIGOROUSLY IN TIME. NOTES ABOVE STAFF: TREBLE; BELOW: BASS; ON: AMBIGUOUS. LINES WERE PART OF COMPOSING MEANS, THE INTERSECTIONS PRODUCING TONES OTHER THAN THE EXTREME PIANO KEYS.

S LIKE C, BUT WITH NOISES: ABOVE LINE = INSIDE PIANO CONSTRUCTION; BELOW = OUTSIDE PIANO CONSTRUCTION.

T INFLUENCES IN PITCH AND TIME NOTATED AS SHAPES WITH CENTER POINTS TO BE AUDIBLE AS CLUSTERS, A SINGLE ONE CHANGING IN ITS COURSE. NUMBERS REFER TO LOUDNESS (1-64) (SOFT TO LOUD OR LOUD TO SOFT)

U CHOOSE ONE OF 3 MUTUALLY EXCLUSIVE AREAS, BOUNDED BY STRAIGHT LINES. PROCEED L. TO R. USING NUMBER OF TONES GIVEN WITHIN DOTTED PARTS.

V PERFORMANCE INDICATIONS ABOVE (READING DOWN) ARE DEGREE OF FORCE, MOST-LEAST; VERTICAL DISTANCE OF ATTACK, FAR-CLOSE; SPEED OF ATTACK, SLOW-FAST. ANY NOISES (BELOW LINE BETWEEN STAVES).

W LEGATO (TRIANGLES) AND STACCATO (ISOLATED NOTES).

X P'S ARE PUNCTUATIONS (BEFORE, AT, DURING, OR END OF INTERVAL THEY ACCOMPANY. ⁒ MEANS REPEAT SOMETHING (OR ALL, OR ANY AMT.) PLAYED BEFORE, BUT CHANGING AMPLITUDE. PEDALS ARE OPTIONAL.

Y 8 PITCH AREAS, CHROMATICALLY ADJACENT, AND HAVING NUMBER OF CHROMATIC TONES GIVEN (LARGE NUMBERS BELOW STAFF). WHEN NOTES ARE ON A LINE, THEY BELONG TO EITHER THE UPPER OR THE LOWER AREA. TIME IN SPACE SECONDS AS INDICATED. LOUDNESS GIVEN BY POSITION OF NOTE WITH RESPECT TO AREA VERTICALLY. HIGH IS fff. LOW IS ppp.

Z CLUSTERS ENDING AS SINGLE TONES. DYNAMICS AS IN T.

AA CLEF AT ALL TIMES AMBIGUOUS. 'STICKS' TO BE PLAYED FREELY (SINGLE TONES, INTERVALS, AGGREGATES, EVENTS, ETC. WITHIN PITCH LIMITS AND RELATIVE TIME LIMITS INDICATED BY THEIR EXTREMITIES (NOTES), USING GRACES AS 'ASSISTANCE'. GIVE EMPHASIS BY DYNAMICS, HARMONICS, REPETITION OR OTHER MEANS TO CIRCLED TONES AND MORE EXTREMELY TO THOSE CIRCLED TWICE OR 3 TIMES.

AB CLUSTERS AS IN Z, SOMETIMES BEGINNING AS SINGLE TONES (NUMBERS ARE DYNAMICS).

AC NOISES. OF THOSE NOTATED PLAY ONLY THAT NUMBER GIVEN. I = INTERIOR PIANO CONSTRUCTION. A = AUXILIARY NOISES. O = OUTER PIANO CONSTRUCTION. THE POSITION OF THE NOTE VERTICALLY GIVES ITS LOUDNESS (HIGH = fff) (LOW IS ppp).

AD SINGLE TONES, INTERVALS AND THREE NOTE AGGREGATES WITH AMBIGUOUS STAFF, LEGER LINES ABOVE, TREBLE, BELOW, BASS.

AE PITCH-TIME AREAS SILENT UNLESS ACCOMPANIED BY NUMBERS, MEANING NUMBER OF TONES (ANY) TO BE PLAYED.

AF EACH EVENT (LINE-CONNECTED NOTES) IS TO BE PLAYED BY ONE HAND ONLY. THE CLEF SIGNS ABOVE ARE FOR THE RIGHT HAND, BELOW FOR THE LEFT.

AG OMIT ANY 2 NOTES OF EACH AGGREGATE.

AH CLEFS FREE (TREBLE OR BASS). HANDS GIVEN. FOLLOW LINES IN DIRECTIONS GIVEN BY ARROWS.

AI PLAY 'WHEEL' OR 'AXLE' USING ONE(S) NOT PLAYED AS HARMONIC(S). PLAY FROM LEFT TO RIGHT.

AJ NUMBERS ARE PROPORTIONAL OF NOTES TO BE PLAYED IN DIRECTIONS GIVEN BY ARROWS CHANGING CLEF AT POINTS WHERE SIGNS APPEAR.

AK PLAY ANY 1 NOTE IN EACH 'UNIVERSE' ACCORDING TO TIME AND AMPLITUDE GIVEN.

AL ANY 8 TONE GAMUT. LARGE NUMBERS ARE PROPORTIONAL TIME BETWEEN SOUND EVENTS. ⌒ = LEGATO . = STACCATO.

AM SINGLE TONES AND INTERVALS EQUAL LENGTHS OF TIME BETWEEN MARKS ABOVE AND BELOW STAFF.

AN CLEFS REFER TO HANDS. FOLLOWING THE LINE FROM LEFT TO RIGHT PLAY ANY NUMBER OF NOTES WITH ONE HAND FOLLOWED BY A DIFFERENT NUMBER WITH LEFT (ETC., IF NUMBERS CHOSEN DO NOT USE ALL THE NOTES).

AO ANY PITCH AREA HAVING AT LEAST 20 CHROMATIC TONES. SPACE VERTICALLY = FREQUENCY, HORIZONTALLY = TIME. HORIZONTAL LINES = DURATION OF SINGLE TONES. VERTICAL LINES = CLUSTERS OR LEGATI. POINTS = SHORT SINGLE TONES.

AP LINES GIVE DURATION. NOTES EQUAL STACCATO.

AQ LIKE Y, BUT USE IN EACH AREA ONLY NOTATIONS ABOVE OR BELOW DOTTED LINE.

AR PLAY IN ANY WAY THAT IS SUGGESTED BY THE DRAWING.

AS A SINGLE NOTE.

AT PERFORM AS IN AE.

AU AS IN Q, BUT EACH LINE HAVING ITS OWN CLEF SIGN BRINGS ABOUT PITCH AMBIGUITY OF SOME OF THE INTERSECTION NOTES.

AV AR WITH THE ADDITION OF NUMBERS GIVING AMPLITUDE (1-64 : fff-ppp OR ppp-fff).

AW SEE AD.

AX NOISES OF ANY AMPLITUDE. BEATERS GIVEN. ON LINES BETWEEN AREAS = 2 BEATERS.

AY GRAPH MUSIC. 1/10 INCH SQUARED = TIME UNIT. NUMBERS WITHIN ARE OF TONES THAT MAY COMPLETE THEIR APPEARANCE WITHIN ANY AMOUNT OF TIME AREA GIVEN THEM BY GRAPH. VERTICAL GRAPH IS FREQUENCY, THE TREBLE AND BASS AREAS MOBILE AS INDICATED.

AZ NUMBERS INDICATE TIME (ANY UNITS). NOTES CONNECTED BY LINES, VERTICAL, ARE CLUSTERS.

BA NUMBERS AS IN T. SOURCES OF NOISE AS IN AC.

BB NOTES ARE SINGLE SOUNDS. LINES ARE DURATION (D), FREQUENCY (F), OVERTONE STRUCTURE (S), AMPLITUDE (A), AND OCCURENCE (SUCCESSION) (O). PROXIMITY TO THESE, MEASURED BY DROPPING PERPENDICULARS FROM NOTES TO LINES GIVES, RESPECTIVELY, LONGEST, LOWEST, SIMPLEST, LOUDEST, AND EARLIEST.

BC PLAY NUMBER OF TONES IN PITCH-AREAS GIVEN. X = ANY NUMBER.

BD NOTES WITH AMPLITUDE GIVEN. ADJACENT AREAS MAY BE USED TO AFFECT ATTACK.

BE NUMBER = EVENTS TO BE EXPRESSED. NOTES REFER TO FINGERS, HANDS, FOREARMS TO BE USED IN PLAYING.

BF NOTES CONNECTED BY LINES TO BE PLAYED LEGATO. SINGLE NOTE = STACCATO. MAKE SUPERIMPOSITIONS AS SUGGESTED BY NOTATION.

BG INTERVALS WITH FREE APPROACHES, DEPARTURES AND SIMULTANEITIES. NUMBERS INDICATE NUMBER OF TONES TO BE PLAYED WITHIN RANGE NOTATED.

BH LIKE A, BUT WITH AMBIGUOUS CLEF.

BI USE 1 OR 2 NUMBERS FOLLOWED BY 1 OR 2 NUMBERS, THE FIRST = FREQUENCIES, THE SECOND, TIME UNITS, CONTINUE OR NOT.

BJ A SINGLE SOUND. BOUNDARIES ARE FREQUENCY, DURATION, AMPLITUDE, AND OVERTONE STRUCTURE. PROXIMITY AS IN BB.

BK LIKE A, BUT WITH NOISES, A, I, AND O AS IN AC (AMPLITUDE FREE).

BL SINGLE NOTES ACCOMPANIED BY NUMBERS GIVING NUMBER OF TONES TO APPEAR ABOVE, BELOW, BEFORE AND AFTER THE ONE NOTATED.

BM PITCHES WITH AMPLITUDE GRAPHICALLY GIVEN. THE HORIZONTAL DIFFERENCE BETWEEN A PITCH AND ITS AMPLITUDE GIVES TIME AVAILABLE FOR TONE.

BN 2 HANDS STARTING AT TWO DIFFERENT POINTS ON PERIMETER ARRIVE EVENTUALLY AT CENTER, TOGETHER, BY ANY PATHS.

BO LIKE W WITH TIME UNITS GIVEN.

BP NUMBERS OF TONES WITHIN RANGES GIVEN FOR EACH HAND.

BQ SINGLE TONES AT ANY POINT (I.E., PITCH, DURATION) WITHIN TRIANGLES. HYPOTENUSE GIVES DYNAMICS AVAILABLE.

BR NUMBER OF TONES THAT MAY BE TAKEN IN ADVANCE FOR PRODUCTION OF HARMONICS GIVEN ABOVE EACH AGGREGATE. PLAY AS IN B.

BS DYNAMICS AS NOTATED FOR BOTH HANDS.

BT NOTES GIVE PLACE OF PERFORMANCE WITH RESPECT TO PIANO.

BU PLAY SOUNDS GIVEN PLUS NUMBER OF SOUNDS WITHIN AREAS. [BETWEEN STAVES = NOISE AREA. ⌴ BELOW = TIME UNITS.

BV THREE LARGE (4 OR MORE SOUNDS), SIX LESS LARGE (3 SOUNDS), 10 SMALL (TWO SOUNDS), 4 VERY SMALL POINTS (SINGLE SOUNDS). THE 5 LINES AND THE 4 BOUNDARIES TO BE USED AS IN BB AND BJ. WHEN OBTAINING MEASUREMENTS FOR 3 FREQUENCIES USE 3 DIFFERENT LINES AND LIKEWISE FOR OTHER MEASUREMENTS.

BW 4 SIDED FIGURES GIVE FREQUENCY, AMPLITUDE, DURATION AND OVERTONE STRUCTURE. THE ILLUSION OF PERSPECTIVE GIVES OCCURENCE, CLOSEST TO THE OBSERVER = EARLIEST IN TIME.

BX ALL AT ONCE LIKE A MOMENT OF A PLANT.

BY ANY NOISES, THEIR RELATIVE PITCH GIVEN GRAPHICALLY (UP = HIGH, DOWN = LOW).

BZ THE 3 PEDALS WITH I = INACTIVITY, AND A = ACTIVITY. ANY OR NO KEYBOARD, HARP OR NOISE SOUNDS.

CA KEYBOARD (WHITE), MUTE (VERTICAL LINES), PIZZ. (BRACKETTED BY DOTTED LINES), AND FRICTION (HORIZONTAL LINES) AREAS GIVEN. NOTES OF ANY PITCH. WHEN AREAS OVERLAP, EITHER, BOTH OR MORE TIMBRES MAY BE PRODUCED.

CB NUMBERS OF TONES IN PITCH AREAS GIVEN

CC THE FOUR DIFFERENTLY DRAWN LINES = FREQUENCY, DURATION, AMPLITUDE, OVERTONE STRUCTURE, IN ANY CORRESPONDANCE. MEASUREMENTS DEFINING THESE ARE TO BE MADE PERPENDICULARLY FROM STRAIGHT LINES ABOVE OR BELOW TO THEIR POINTS OF INTERSECTION WITH SLANTING LINES. NUMBERS AT ENDS OF THESE GIVE BY THEIR DIFFERENCE TIME AVAILABLE FOR SOUNDS.

CD FOR . USE 1 OF 4 READINGS. FOR o USE 2 OF 4 READINGS. FOR X USE 3 OF 4 READINGS. HORIZONTAL READINGS = KEYBOARD. VERTICAL READINGS = HARP.

CE CLEFS AMBIGUOUS. LEGER LINES ABOVE 𝄢 = 15, BELOW 𝄞 = 13. MAKE INTERVALS AND AGGREGATES WHERE SUGGESTED BY NOTATION.

CF AS IN BZ.

3/27/58.

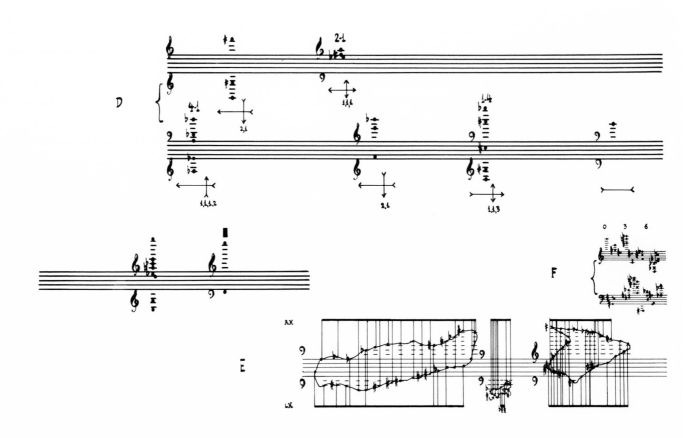

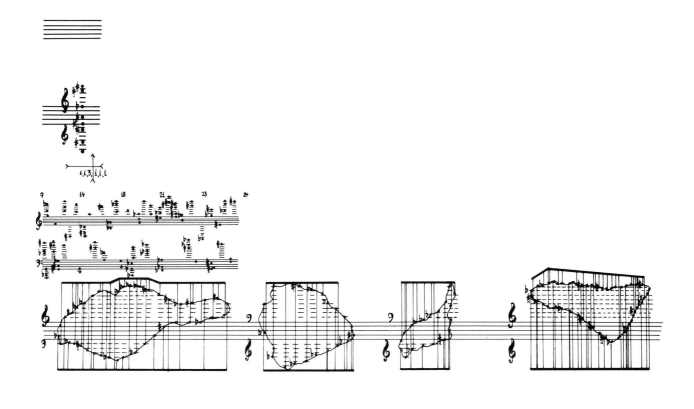

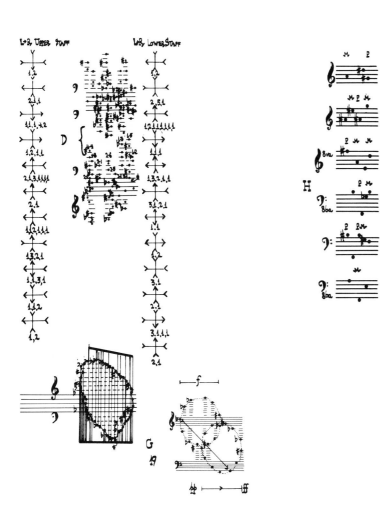

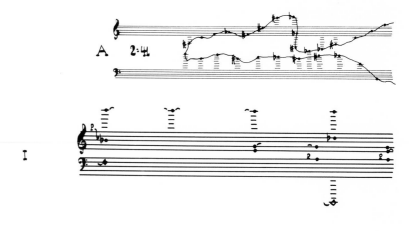

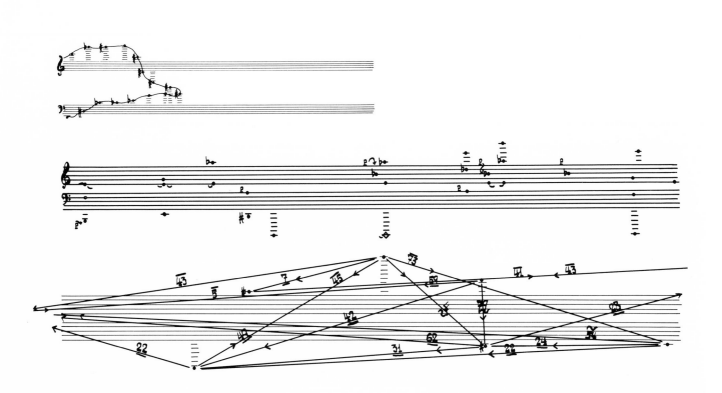

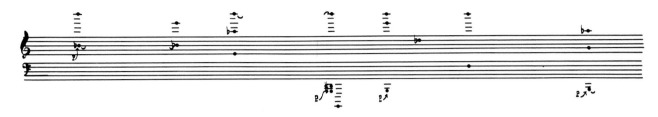

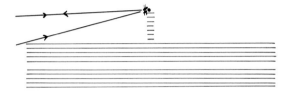

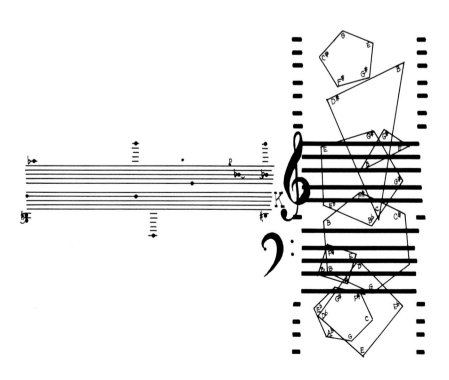

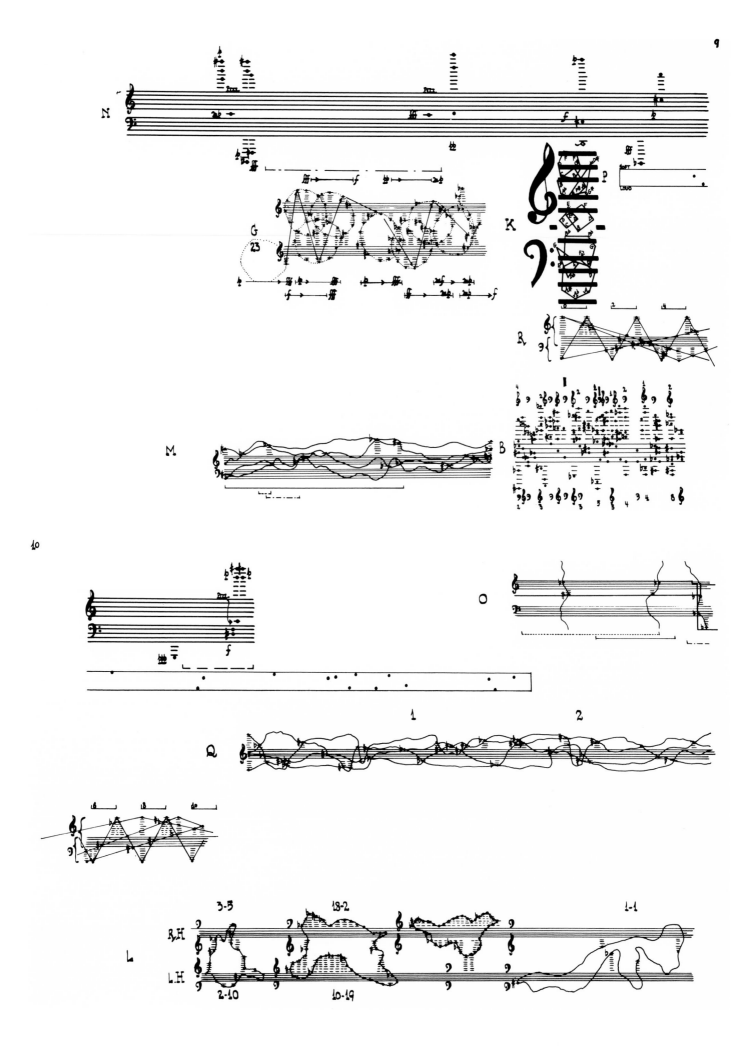

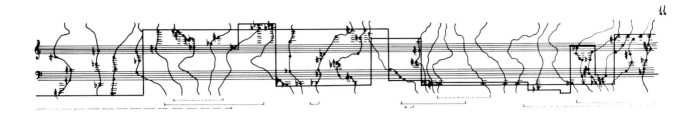

3   4   (5)

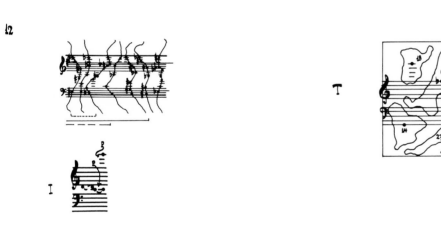

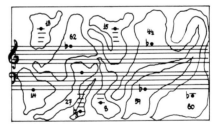

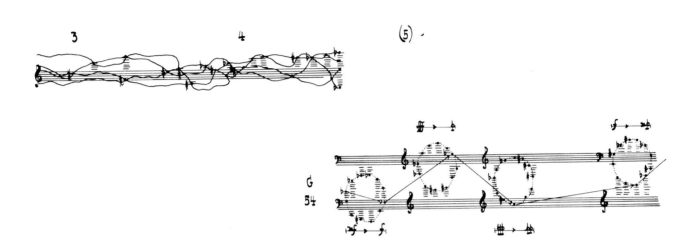

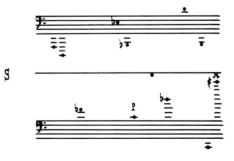

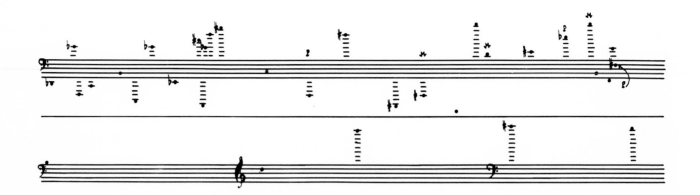

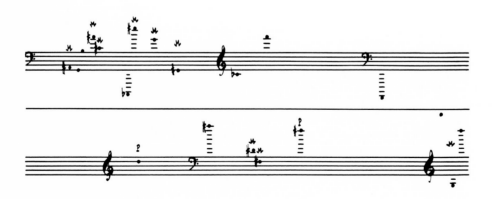

Points in Space

I

This exhibition of the holograph of the 63 pages forming the piano part of Cage's Concert for Piano and Orchestra (1957-58) is more or less the equivalent of an exhibition of a set of architectural plans for a particular building and its grounds. However beautiful and interesting it may be to look at, it was not made as something to be looked at. It was made as a set of instructions for a construction to be realised by someone (the performer, the builder): the forms it presents and their relative placings are determined by the composer's desire to communicate his requirements to the performer as effectively as possible. There are, of course, when writing music, often alternative ways of communicating something to the performer, and it is not inconceivable that, where such alternatives presented themselves here, even Cage, with his attachment to the principle of rejecting opportunities to indulge personal aesthetic preferences, was not beyond instinctively choosing those he liked the look of.

The simple reason for which, in the first place, I have compared these pages with architectural plans, rather than with some other kind of diagram which conveys instructions for making or assembling something, is the way they mix the rectilinear and the curvilinear, with biomorphic lines or figures, like plans for winding paths or lakes or areas of parkland, placed here and there among the dominant sets of parallel straight lines. But there is a far deeper similarity than that. In an architectural drawing the relative magnitude of the lines is in proportion to the relative magnitude of the things they represent: if the east and west walls in the plan of a building are two-thirds the length of the north and south walls, so will they be in the building. But where, in a traditional musical score, three consecutive pages are packed with runs of demi-semiquavers and are followed, with no change of tempo, by three consecutive pages of minims and crotchets, the first three pages are going to be played in a small fraction of the time it takes to play the second three. This is because the notation uses the position of a note on the stave only to indicate its pitch, not its duration; the duration is indicated by a semiotic convention. Cage, however, has invented a notation in which the duration of notes is not indicated by a code; the notes are all tailless and their duration is indicated by their relative placing within the page. Thus a page that is blank (e.g., page 15) is manifestly one of those infamous periods of silence. Manifestly. The measure here of time is space.

What is not manifest in the pages of the Concert for Piano and Orchestra is how the performer is supposed to deal with a given configuration. This is where a code is used, a code that is explained in the prefatory pages. It consists of 84 letters or combinations of letters one of which is placed before each configuration of notes. For instance, the letter A (e.g., pages 1, 5-6) means: 'Following the perimeter, from any note on it, play in opposite directions in the proportion given. Here and elsewhere, the absence of indications of any kind means freedom for the performer in that regard.' Or, again, the letter G (e.g., pages 4, 9, 11-12) means: 'Of notes written play number given in any manner (keys, harp) beginning and ending as indicated by arrow. Dynamic indications accompany each circle on the circumference of which the notes are placed. (Scale ppp-fff)'. A large part of the instructions has to do with telling the performer where he is free to act according to his own choice. In Cage's mature music a performer is not an 'interpreter', someone trying to convey what someone else wants to say; he is a co-composer, sharing the decisions on what to say. And along with that constant interaction between the composer's decisions and the performer's, the music also crucially involves interaction with decisions provided by chance operations, such as throwing dice.

For any performance of the Concert the variables to be determined by the performers and/or chance include how much of the music is to be performed, the length of time in which each configuration is to be performed, and which of the possible performers is actually going to perform. The maximum instrumentation consists of piano, three violins, two violas, 'cello, double bass, flute, clarinet, bassoon (or baritone saxophone), trumpet, trombone, tuba and a voice, plus a conductor who is no less optional (and whose role, when present, is not to mark beats but to use his arms like a clock, to measure the length of time within which a certain sequence of notes is to be played). There was at least one occasion when the freedom of choice served a high humanitarian purpose. At the first rehearsal of a full orchestral performance in the South of France, the excellent trombonist, a Japanese, fluffed a difficult top F. His sense of shame was distressing to behold. And then at the second rehearsal he fluffed the note again. He vowed that, if this happened in the performance, he was going to commit hara-kiri, and his colleagues knew him well enough to be alarmed. Cage, however, who was conducting, cooled matters by saying decisively that, while the trombonist was to perform in the other works to be played that evening, the Concert for Piano and Orchestra would have its trombone part omitted. It became clear that the trombonist took this as a well-meaning insult to his honour when, shortly after the rehearsal ended, it was found that he had disappeared, together with his instrument, and that a long-bladed knife was also missing. His colleagues hurried out to the woods to look for him. There was no sign of him until they heard the note, coming through the trees, perfectly formed. The trombone part was still left out of the performance.

'The Concert for Piano and Orchestra is without a master score, but each part is written in detail in a notation where space is relative to time determined by the performer and later altered by a conductor. Both specific directives and specific freedoms are given to each player including the conductor. Notes are of three sizes referring ambiguously to duration or amplitude. As many various uses of the instruments as could be discovered were subjected to the composing means which involved chance operations and the observation of imperfections in the paper upon which the music was written. The pianist's part is a ''book'' containing 84 different kinds of composition, some, varieties of the same species, others, altogether different. The pianist is free to play any elements of his choice, wholly or in part and in any sequence.'

That summary description of the work by the composer reveals, directly or by analogy, a good deal about what Cage stands for and is. But then there are few things more revealing about anyone than clues as to where and how they impose demands upon others and where and how they let others pursue their own course. And as to when and where they stop trying to control things and let chance take over.

Three years ago, when an exhibition of contemporary music manuscripts was on at the Serpentine Gallery, I went to see it with my friend Diego Masson. I took advantage of his having conducted a high percentage of the works by questioning him as to whether the scores which appeared to me to be the likeliest for a conductor to find difficult actually were. But we also talked about scores as objects for looking at, and he remarked, making it clear that he was thinking of past as much as present music, 'A score which is beautiful to look at usually sounds better than one which is not'.

The chances of a Cage score's being beautiful to look at are presumably increased by his having had a history as a painter. After dropping out of Pomona College at the age of seventeen, he went to Paris and stayed for six months, long enough to see a good deal of modern art and hear some modern music. 'The impression I gained was that, if that was the way things were, I could do it too.' Then, in the course of a year's wandering around Europe and North Africa, he started painting and writing and composing, and he went on with them all when he moved back to Los Angeles. He painted landscapes from the motif, in a way somewhat influenced by Van Gogh, and then he painted what he saw in reflections in spherical surfaces such as the chromium part of car headlights – reflections in them of architecture, yielding simple forms transformed by the optical distortion. This led to his painting invented abstract shapes. 'And what was interesting to me then was to make a very thin application of the oil on canvas, and to make it by using, not a brush, but steel wool, so that I was rubbing the paint onto the surface of the canvas.' From the start, then, Cage was fascinated by the use of new or uncommon procedures. The great innovators in the arts can be divided into those who are primarily inventors of new forms and those who like Cage are primarily inventors of new procedures. Primarily. New forms lead to new procedures and vice versa.

Cage's versatile youth came to an abrupt end when he was twenty-two and asked Schönberg to give him lessons. Schönberg did not mind his not being able to pay but did insist that he promise to devote his life to music. (Schönberg, of course, knew what he was talking about, having himself been a considerable painter.) Cage, ever mindful of that promise, produced no further work of visual art till 1969. In the meantime, though, music of his had been exhibited as visual art. It was, indeed, the music exhibited here. The time was May 1958, when a retrospective concert of Cage's music was staged at the New York Town Hall and concluded (ultimately in uproar) with the first performance, conducted by Merce Cunningham, of the Concert for Piano and Orchestra. In celebration, the pages of the piano part were exhibited in the upstairs room at the Stable Gallery (while Rauschenberg was having a show downstairs). Several of the pages were sold; Cage wrote them out again to keep the set complete.

It was because of seeing some manuscript of Cage's that Alice Weston was moved to ask him to produce a graphic work in memory of Marcel Duchamp. This was what finally made him break the promise to Schönberg; he produced a series of plexigrams. Three years later he made ten lithographs for a mycological book of which he was co-author. He was becoming increasingly mindful now of Margaret Mead's view that, living much longer as we do, we have the opportunity to live, not just one life, but several. In 1978 he decided to accept an invitation from Kathan Brown of the Crown Point Press in Oakland to come out there and experiment with making prints. Since taking that decision he has published about twenty albums of etchings or monotypes and has also produced a quantity of drawings, made in 1984 and '87. They are works whose interest is independent of Cage's greatness as a composer and importance as a writer; indeed, it seems to me that the best of them – for instance, the series of four drypoints, *Where R=Ryoanji*, of 1983 – are among the most beautiful prints and drawings made anywhere in the '80s.

Now that that material exists, the piano part of the Concert for Piano and Orchestra is seen in an art gallery very differently from how it was in 1958. It is now the equivalent of a set of architectural plans by an architect who is also established as an artist. Cage himself has elected to show it, rather than recent prints or drawings, for his first exhibition in London, perhaps because of the exhibition's context. A reason for welcoming his decision is that pages of music represent his central activity. And they do certainly present, if with less immediacy, the qualities which radiate from the drawings and prints. 'Radiate' is exact, because the supreme quality of these works is how they contain light. That a drawing should do this is, of course, a criterion of its quality. At the same time, Cage's music as I listen seems to be peculiarly analogous to light. All that Cage does seems filled with light. Light and also lightness – for one thing, because of his way of making everything he does look effortless.

The immediate satisfaction I get from the piano part of the Concert is a sense of the grace with which the configurations sit or lie here and there upon the page. They do so, incidentally, in a way that reflects Cage's love of using collage – 'the bringing together of things that wouldn't be together unless you brought them together' – whatever the medium he is working in. In this manuscript he was not physically using collage, but he was thinking in collage terms, it seems to me, inasmuch as I have a feeling in looking at the page that each of the configurations there existed independently of all the others before being placed upon it. This feeling is accompanied by a concentrated awareness of the exact dimensions of the page, a pleasure in the finality of its edges. Till suddenly the sheet of yellowing paper disappears, ceases to be a surface and becomes a space, a space for the enactment of a dance – a dance which arises for the simple reason that in these pages space means time, distances mark beats.

The dance that unfolds is a vivid interaction between movements that are regular, formal, rigorous, and movements that are fluid and meandering. It makes me think of Morris dancing and its intense contrast between the disciplined, compact, frontal movements in a rectilinear framework – an extreme order, a violent order – of the six (or eight) dancers forming what is called the set and, winding in and out of that order, the wayward, unpredictable movements of the Hobby-horse and the Fool (or the transvestite figure called the Betsy). That dance, it seems to me, is a paradigm of the dialectic which underlies how all art operates. In Cage's work – and in the work of Cunningham and of Johns – this is not merely there below the surface. It is the overt guiding principle, the subject-matter almost, this play between the given and the indeterminate.

David Sylvester

MERCE CUNNINGHAM

Born Centralia, Washington 1919

Merce Cunningham with Martha Graham in *El Penitente*, 1940

Merce Cunningham teaching at Black Mountain College, North Carolina, 1948

Carolyn Brown, Merce Cunningham and Barbara Lloyd in *Suite for Five in Time and Space*, 1956

Merce Cunningham in *Antic Meet*, 1958

Merce Cunningham with Carolyn Brown in *Night Wandering*, 1958

Merce Cunningham, Carolyn Brown and Steve Paxton in *Aeon*, 1961

Merce Cunningham in *How to Pass, Kick, Fall and Run*, 1965

Merce Cunningham in *Walkaround Time*, 1968. Design by Jasper Johns, based on *The Large Glass* by Marcel Duchamp

Merce Cunningham and Carolyn Brown at Westbeth rehearsing duet from *Suite for Five*, 1972

Merce Cunningham and Company with John Cage at Westbeth rehearsing *Second Hand*, 1970

Merce Cunningham and Karole Armitage in *Squaregame*, 1976

Merce Cunningham, 1981

Merce Cunningham

'Dancing, for me,' Merce Cunningham has said, 'is movement in time and space.' If this statement sounds obvious, that is because Cunningham has made us look at dancing that way. His choreography is concerned with the fact of movement, as the music of John Cage is concerned with the fact of sound, or a painting by Jasper Johns with the fact of a certain object. Where other choreographers may find their motivation, or 'inspiration', in a piece of music, or in a literary or psychological theme, Cunningham starts, as he puts it, with a step, a movement that may be the seed of an entire work. (He is fond of the story of the great tap dancer, 'Honi' Coles, calling his mentor, John Bubbles, and being asked, 'Have you made any new steps?')

In the first pieces Cunningham and Cage made together in the early forties, dance and music shared an agreed time structure, coming together only at key points. By the early fifties, this was carried to its logical conclusion – the two elements co-existing, but independently, with no relation except simultaneity of occurrence.

Creation, for Cunningham, is not a matter of inspiration; as is well known, he uses chance operations to plot the sequence of phrases in a dance and to determine such other factors as where they will be performed in the space, and by how many dancers. This process enables him to discover ways of moving that he might not have thought of if he had relied on habit or intuition.

It follows that Cunningham does not accept conventional ways of using space. He rejects configurations derived from the Renaissance theory of perspective, as in classic ballet, where the action radiates from a central point, the ballerina, supported by her partner and the successive ranks of coryphées and corps de ballet. Even in the modern dance, there was a belief that certain areas of the stage were 'stronger' than others (as proposed in Doris Humphrey's *The Art of Making Dances*). Cunningham decided early on that no one point was more important than another, that each individual dancer could be the centre of the space he or she occupied.

This notion of a multiplicity of centres could be called a Zen concept, though Cunningham's study of Zen was not as thorough as Cage's; it is also clearly analogous to the organization of the pictorial space in much contemporary painting. Cunningham himself says that where he found confirmation was in Einstein's statement, 'There are no fixed points in space.'

*

For the most part, Cunningham's radical formal innovations have been arrived at pragmatically rather than theoretically, as the result of the necessity to deal with a particular problem or situation. In 1952, he was invited by Leonard Bernstein to choreograph two works for a Festival of the Creative Arts at Brandeis University, Waltham, Massachusetts. One was a version of Stravinsky's *Les Noces*, which he choreographed in a more or less conventional way, following the dramatic and musical structure.

The other was the first piece of *musique concrète* to be played in the United States, Pierre Schaeffer's *Symphonie pour un homme seul*. Excerpts from this were to be played twice at the concert, because of their unfamiliarity, but Cunningham decided against repeating the same choreography. Instead, he made a solo for himself and a group dance using several experienced dancers who had been studying with him in New York as well as a number of Brandeis students with very little training. He had lately begun to work with chance processes, finding ways to apply to choreography the kind of operations Cage was using in music. Cunningham drew up three gamuts of possible movements: one consisting of phrases that he had invented, a second consisting of movements from social dances, and a third consisting of everyday movements and gestures. Thus, for the first time Cunningham was using non-dance movement, not for a mimetic purpose, but as an element in choreography, and his primary reason for doing so was to make available movements within the capabilities of the untrained students.

Similarly, the sounds out of which this piece of music on electronic tape were constructed could not be counted by the dancers in the usual way. Cunningham therefore decided simply to make a dance of the same time-length as the music, with no attempt to relate dance and music. From that time on, most of his dances have been made in time-lengths in this way.

In 1964, during the Merce Cunningham Dance Company's six-month world tour, Cunningham was invited to perform at the Museum des 20.Jahrhunderts in Vienna. There was no theatre in the museum, but he was told that a platform could be built and some kind of stage rigged up. Cunningham instead decided to make a piece consisting of excerpts from the repertory put together in a new sequence, which could be performed in an open space in the museum before a wall of windows looking out on to a public park. He called the piece *Museum Event No. 1*. Later in the tour two further *Museum Events* were given in the Moderna Museet in Stockholm. Cunningham liked the result, both for the way in which it allowed him to recycle choreographic material and for the possibility it afforded of performing in a non-theatrical space. Many of the theatres in which his company performed were inadequate in one way or another, but often a better space might be available in a gymnasium, an arena, or even out of doors. Since 1964, his company has performed hundreds of *Events* in such venues.

*

It is clear that Cunningham has long since abandoned the usual principles governing dance structure: cause and effect, conflict and resolution, building to a climax, are things that simply do not occur in his dances. Yet in recent years many observers have detected a 'new' narrative element in Cunningham's work, just as others have found his movement increasingly balletic. The fact is that Cunningham's work has always been dramatic in a certain sense – and there have always been similarities to classic ballet in his movement.

When he first went to the Cornish School in Seattle, in 1937, it was to study theatre – it was only after he began to study modern dance there with Bonnie Bird that he realised that theatre for him meant dance, and switched his course of studies accordingly. But he has always been a consummate actor with a commanding stage presence, which remains true now that the amount of actual movement he can perform is limited.

83

The juxtaposition of the ageing Cunningham with his company of young virtuosi in itself creates a dramatic situation; it was hard not to see the harrowing *Quartet* as a meditation on his own death. In his brief passages across the stage in recent works, Cunningham appears as a Prospero- or Lear-like figure; the other side of the coin is his Beckett-like persona in comedy works such as *Roadrunners*, *Gallopade*, and *Grange Eve* – as W C Fields said, 'I never saw anything funny that wasn't terrible.'

Such dances as the three chance solos from the fifties, *Untitled Solo*, *Lavish Escapade*, and *Changeling*, were dramatic of their own intensity. The 1960 dance *Crises* was very clearly about a man's often stormy relationships with four women. The vaudeville element has always been present, in such works as *Antic Meet* (1958), to Cage's Concert for Piano and Orchestra, whose epigraph was from *The Brothers Karamazov*: 'Let me tell you that the absurd is only too necessary on earth.'

Cunningham never goes even that far in terms of a programme note nowadays (though his titles are as evocative as any in contemporary dance); he certainly never spells out a dance's meaning. He and Cage believe in Duchamp's apophthegm that the spectator completes the work of art – it is for the spectator to make interpretations of the dances, or not. What Cunningham cares about is that the spectators look at, really *see* the dances, not try to figure out what they might or might not mean. More to the point, really, is that Cunningham's work, like Cage's, 'imitates nature in the manner of her operation', or as Cunningham himself has put it, imitates 'the way nature makes a space and puts lots of things in it, heavy and light, little and big, all unrelated, yet each affecting all the others'. As Alastair Macaulay said to me recently, his dances 'keep returning us to life and the world'.

As for Cunningham's dance technique, it is based on the simplest of principles: he once told a student that dancing consists of changing the weight from one foot to the other. Cunningham originally started teaching in order to train dancers to move in the way he wanted: dancers from other modern dance studios either could not do so or else wanted to know their motivation, something he wasn't interested in telling them. He had studied for a while at Balanchine's School of American Ballet; in developing his own technique he combined the leg action and the pelvic turn-out

84

of ballet with the flexibility of the torso of the modern dance. In recent years Cunningham has become more and more interested in virtuosity, and has trained his dancers to move with preternatural speed, lightness, and precision.

*

When he studied at the old School of American Ballet on Madison Avenue and 59th Street, Cunningham used to visit the nearby art galleries between classes. Later he and Cage became friendly with the painters of the New York School. (It was at Cage's suggestion that Willem and Elaine de Kooning were invited to Black Mountain College in North Carolina in the summer of 1948.) The painters were the most loyal audience for early concerts by Cunningham and Cage. But it was with Robert Rauschenberg and Jasper Johns that they felt a closer kinship: seeing Rauschenberg's all-white paintings in the summer of 1952 encouraged Cage to write his famous 'silent' piece, 4′33″.

From 1954 to 1964 Cunningham collaborated with Rauschenberg; after a brief interregnum Johns became Artistic Adviser to the Dance Company, designing several dances himself but otherwise selecting painters who he thought 'could understand a difference between theatre and studio'. Rauschenberg rarely and Johns never imposed their vision on Cunningham's choreography – their objective was not to 'get in the way' of the dancers. (Mark Lancaster continued to work on the same lines when he became resident designer in the early seventies.)

Cunningham, for his part, always allowed the painters a free hand, within certain practical limits – the principle was the same as with the composers. The painters Johns brought in often modified the stage space in some way: Frank Stella with his moveable strips of canvas in primary colours for *Scramble*, Andy Warhol with his silver mylar pillows for *RainForest* (originally a gallery installation, 'Silver Clouds'), Robert Morris with his column that moved back and forth at the front of the stage for *Canfield*, Bruce Nauman with his row of industrial fans, also set between dancers and audience, for *Tread*. Cunningham's response was to deal with the situation, as with any other practical problem.

Johns always preferred not to make a set, except in the case of *Walkaround Time*, for which he adapted Marcel Duchamp's *The Large Glass*, reproducing the images on a number of clear plastic 'boxes'. Otherwise, the most he would do was to provide a backcloth of a particular colour to offset the costumes. (Again, this principle was followed by Lancaster in his designs.) He has said that he felt that 'each dance should have its own distinctive costumes'. But they too were always unobtrusive: the costumes for *Second Hand* were dyed in such a way that they formed a spectrum, but this was evident only when the dancers lined up across the stage for their final bow.

The closest Johns ever came to a design that could be called spectacular was in *Un jour ou deux*, the ballet that Cunningham and Cage made for the Paris Opéra in 1973. He used the full depth of the huge stage of the Opéra, cutting it in two, with two gauze curtains, shading from light to dark grey, one at the proscenium and one half-way back. First the space between the two scrims, and then the space behind the second one, were gradually made visible with back-lighting, revealing the shadowy shapes of the masonry of the rear wall of the stage.

Un jour ou deux, like *Aeon* (designed by Rauschenberg, with music by Cage) and *Exchange* (designed by Johns, with music by David Tudor), was one of Cunningham's epic works, in which whole epochs seemed to pass before one's eyes. Johns's designs for *Exchange* were in sombre greys, with touches of sooty colour at the edges of the backcloth and the costumes; a costume he made for Cunningham with pockets in which various objects were to be placed was never used, because Johns himself felt it to be too intrusive.

*

In the last fifteen years Cunningham has extended his collaboration to film and video, working first with Charles Atlas and then with Elliot Caplan, resident filmmakers with the Cunningham Dance Foundation. Nearly all of Cunningham's work in these media has been in the form of dances choreographed for the camera, rather than of previous pieces 'reconceived'. Contrary to the usual practice, he has in most cases later reworked them for stage presentation. He recognised in his first tentative experiments that the space seen by the camera differs from that seen by the spectator in a theatre : a triangle that widens from the camera aperture as opposed to a rectangle that narrows. His decentralization of the space in his theatre choreography has enabled him to deal with this situation, just as working in precise time-lengths has enabled him to deal with the necessity for such limitations in television.

For both stage and screen, Cunningham's output has been astonishingly prolific in recent years. In 1989 alone, he has choreographed four new works: *Cargo X*, *Field and Figures*, *Inventions*, and *August Pace*, all company works with no role for himself. In earlier dances in which he does appear, his presence is riveting; he may be able to do less, but he finds more and more ways to do it. His hands flutter about him like hummingbirds – his gestures are as precise and as powerful as his leaps once were. And the dances he makes for his company are full of beauty, fantasy, and surprise. At the age of seventy, Cunningham's 'appetite for motion' is as voracious as ever.

David Vaughan

JASPER JOHNS

Born Augusta, Georgia 1930

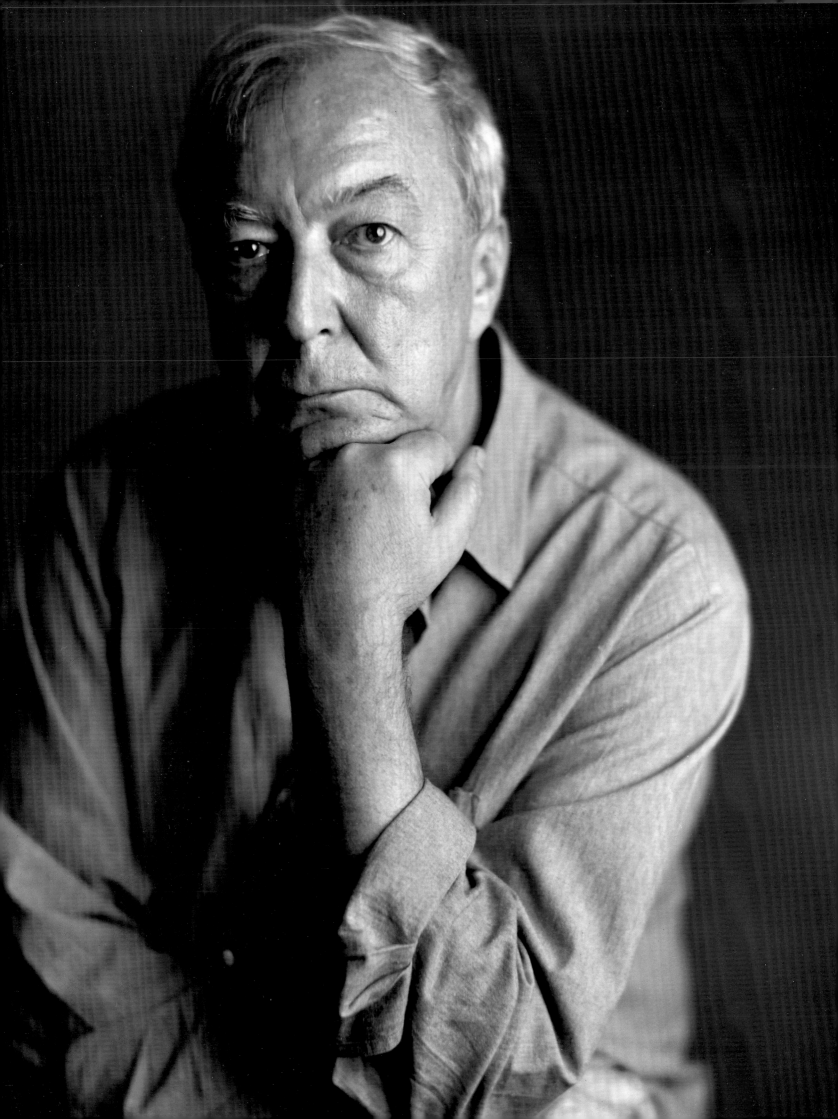

1 *Cicada* 1979 $38\frac{1}{2} \times 28$ inches

2 *Cicada* 1979 $30\frac{1}{2}\times 22$ inches

3 *Dancers on a Plane* 1979 $77\frac{7}{8} \times 64$ inches

4 *Dancers on a Plane* 1980 $78\frac{3}{8} \times 63\frac{3}{4}$ inches

5 *Dancers on a Plane* 1980-81 $29\frac{7}{8} \times 23\frac{3}{4}$ inches

6 *Dancers on a Plane* 1982 35 × 27 inches

7 *Tantric Detail* 1980 58×41 inches

8 *Tantric Detail I* 1980 50⅛ × 34⅛ inches

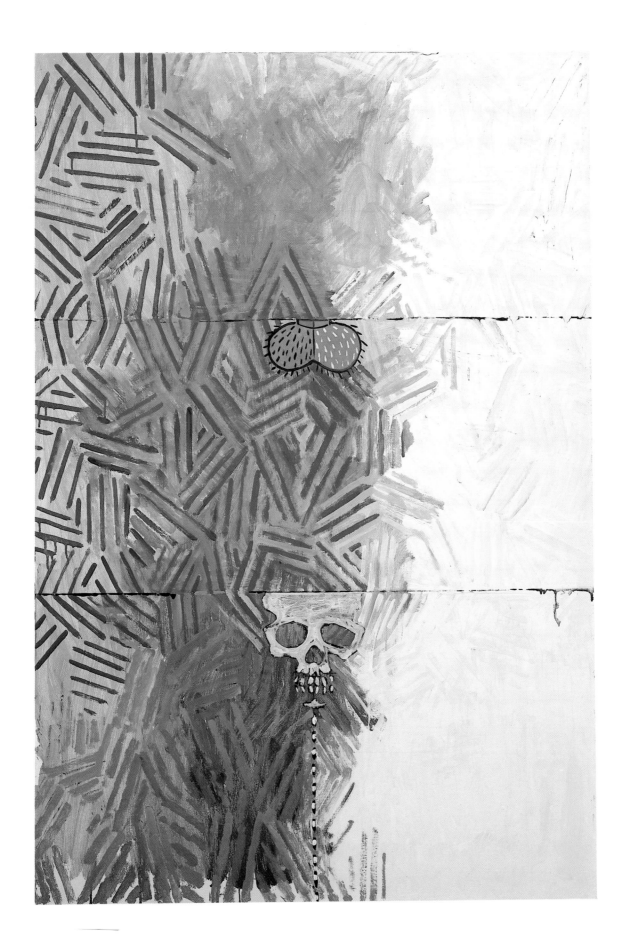

10 *Tantric Detail III* 1981 $50\frac{1}{8} \times 34\frac{1}{8}$ inches

9 *Tantric Detail II* 1981 50⅛ × 34⅛ inches

11 *Usuyuki (Study for Merce Cunningham Minneapolis Residency Poster)* 1981 $36\frac{1}{4} \times 57$ inches

12 *Between the Clock and the Bed* 1981 22¼ × 31 inches

1981 72 × 126¼ inches

14 *Perilous Night* 1982 $31\frac{5}{8} \times 40\frac{7}{8}$ inches

Dancers on a Plane and other stratagems
for inclusion in the work of Jasper Johns

There is much on Jasper Johns's mind: his works are dense with referential material, surface complexity, and strategies about the making of art. In his hands, the work of art is greatly manipulatable: it is subject to all kinds of operations that extend its boundaries, and can be pushed and bullied into accepting new definitions and identities. As his career evolved, Johns gradually synthesized a bewitching range of experiences, and the work of art became a container for a set of effects, some of which might be viewed as unconventional in art, others of which enabled him to further his personal aesthetic reach.

The springboard for Johns's exploration is his recognition that the world is overflowing with objects. Given that framework, he asks himself how art relates to this superfluidity, interweaving traditional notions of art with contemporary conceptions that view it as just another thing in the world, one more object, which shares all the qualities of prosaic existence. He brings this somewhat paradoxical situation to the fore, and plays on the confusion that results: does the work of art presume to attain 'objecthood' or does it remain a fictional construction that only pretends to hold the status that actual objects have, or does it partake of both?[1]

Once Johns has altered the work of art so as to include within its boundaries qualities that all objects share, the viewer must confront a number of issues that experience in life teaches: preconceptions can be misleading, and one must question the nature of an object, its physical and psychological characteristics. From Johns's standpoint, a crucial circumstance is that every object has an unseen inner space. 'I think,' he explains, 'that our main conception of an object is that it will hold something.'[2] If one recognizes that there is an interior to a work by Johns, the viewer must then discover what it holds or it might disclose, and what the appearance of its contents is.

Johns is almost preoccupied with this, and describes his concern in various ways: 'One of the extreme problems of paintings as objects is the other side – the back.

Fig. 1 *Target with Plaster Casts*, 1955
(See page 135 for details of all figures)

Fig. 2 *Souvenir 2*, 1964

It can't be solved; it's in the nature of the work.'[3] Since something is almost always at least partially unseen, he will often emphasize fragments in his work,[4] and has observed the need to distinguish between parts and a whole.[5] Because objects are rarely if ever fully revealed or revealing, his decisions while making a picture may therefore be determined, not by what he has just done there, but 'by what is not on the canvas'.[6] These are not only questions regarding a physical relationship of parts; a psychological dimension exists as well.[7]

Given this conundrum, the spectator may come to feel that a work by Johns cannot be fully understood, and that the creator of it is in a perfect position to hide its contents, or to create a situation in which only selective aspects can be discerned. This air of mystery has, of course, been central to Johns's art from the start. Often in his earliest work, for example *Target with Plaster Casts*, 1955 (fig. 1),[8] he depicts two kinds of spaces, each with very different information. The juxtaposition itself causes bewilderment, although it is now apparent that we are observing disparate sides of the same thing, with the likelihood that there is yet more which is beyond our view. Even when the subject is complete and given in a fairly deadpan way, as in Johns's renderings of flags or numbers, one is challenged; these images just seem to be permeated with an unseen something. The fact, for instance, that one can often glimpse fragments of collaged newsprint beneath the painted surface is a means for Johns to hint that there is, indeed, more to be learned. In *Souvenir 2*, 1964 (fig. 2), he acknowledged that something does lie behind the painting, and with the aid of a flashlight and a rearview mirror (rearview being a literal reference), we discover an image of Johns himself ostensibly sequestered on the back of his canvas.

If the work of art holds surprises, then it is important to learn the methods by which these might be discovered. Johns entices us to employ more than one sense in the process of appreciating and apprehending his objects.[9] Obviously, looking is central to and characteristic of art, but Johns creates so many trick and double images, inkblot patterns, and fragmentary apparitions that the viewer's sense of vision is tested to its limits. He also creates devices that call the mind into play, as well.

Not all of Johns's sensory games or inclusions are literal, although being a literal

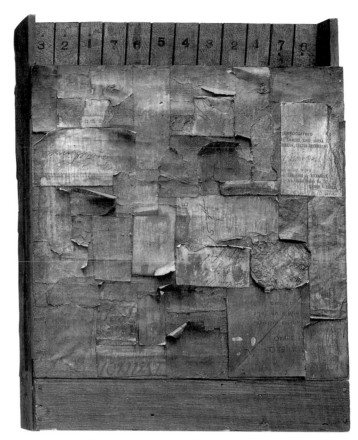

Fig. 3 *Construction with Toy Piano*, 1954

Fig. 4 *Tango*, 1955

minded person, he probably prefers that situation. Still, he is willing to accept a theoretical context, and expects that the viewer concurs, for that, after all, is natural to the illusionistic history of art.[10] For instance, by duplicating the patterns on the edges of adjoining canvases, in a multi-panel work, he suggested that the canvases could be overlapped to form a new structure, without losing any information.[11] Elsewhere, with the marks painted at the vertical edges of a single canvas, he implied that an overall composition is continuous, and that it might have been intended to cover a cylindrical form.[12] But, since the stretchers for these paintings do not actually allow for such possibilities, Johns is assuming a conceptual or theoretical point of view in order to show what might be accomplished. He is fascinated with the mental exercises that can be applied to perceptions of the canvas object, both on his part and that of the viewer.[13] For him, art is always a game of sorts, with rules, systems, and logical proceedings, all of which may be contradicted, 'adulterated or abused' at any time.[14]

Above all Johns depends on the involvement of the spectator who, in effect, 'completes' the work. Johns's various and devious inclusions and plays on the nature of art are designed for the delectation and confusion of the observer. In this regard, one should recall his perplexing tale of a 'spy' (the artist) and 'watchman' (the viewer),[15] both of whom live in the space of the work of art, and are aware of one another. One of the earliest known works by Johns is *Construction with Toy Piano*, 1954 (fig. 3), in which a set of keys from a child's piano tempts the observer to touch the piece.[16] The artist quickly followed this with other objects that courted the viewer's involvement, including *Tango*, 1955 (fig. 4), in which a key at the lower right operates a music box attached to the back of the canvas. In *Target with Plaster Casts*, he mimics the piano keys with irregular slats on hinges, which again issue an invitation; here, however, instead of making music, one opens a Pandora's box of sorts. Not plagues but body parts, cast from a human being, are uncovered, to shock the unsuspecting.

The degree to which the early works are conceived in terms of viewer participation and reaction indicates the significance of these aspects to Johns's developing concept of the nature of art. For instance, regarding a work entitled *Target with Four Faces*, 1955, he said: 'I thought that what one saw would change as one moved toward the painting, and that one might notice the change and be aware of moving and touching and causing sound or changing what was visible. In such a complex of activity, the painting became something other than a simplified image.'[17] Not only did Johns want to add certain experiences to the nature of art, he even sought to influence the specific physical movements and perceptions of the viewer during his perambulation. However, continuing in the same statement, the artist indicated the weakness in his strategy, that soon after the works left his possession, they would have no longer been accessible to the actual touch of very many if any spectators, especially if the objects entered museums.[18] Therefore, *Drawer*, 1957 (Brandeis University Collection), and *Shade*, 1959 (Ludwig Collection, Aachen), which both tempt participation, are not actually constructed to function, as were the earlier works. However, if tempted to touch or participate in the 'game', the viewer would be frustrated by the inoperable nature of these works, which once more indicates that Johns was planning for an observer's response.[19]

In an often told story, Johns was introduced to Marcel Duchamp's work in the mid-1950s by his friend Robert Rauschenberg, and subsequently visited the Philadelphia Museum of Art to see the extensive repository of Duchamp's objects there. Discovering Duchamp must have been one of the great revelations of Johns's life, in as much as the Dadaist's art reaffirmed certain directions he had already taken.[20] Johns proceeded to write about Duchamp on a number of occasions, remarking that his attacks on conventional notions of art were especially to be admired,[21] that Duchamp had moved art past 'retinal boundaries . . . into a field where language, thought and vision act upon one another',[22] and that he had shown how an art work and observer occupy the same place in time.[23] These ideas would, of course, have made great sense to Johns, who was already pursuing viewer participation, evolving a concept of art that was perplexing for all its literalness, and strengthening the importance of language and thought in visual art. For both Duchamp and Johns, art was clearly something more than an object conceived within a narrowly-defined framework, which is stared at and dispensed with.

Duchamp had created numerous works which solicit viewer participation, and offer stimulation beyond the visual,[24] works which certainly must have had an influence on Johns. For example, with its transparency, *The Large Glass* (Philadelphia Museum of Art) had the capacity to include or contain part of the room in which it is installed as integral to its nature. For his sculpture *With Hidden Noise*, 1916 (Philadelphia Museum of Art), Duchamp asked his friend and patron Walter Arensberg to secrete an object within, and not to identify it even to him; only when the work was shaken and the object made a noise would its presence be revealed. Duchamp's cunning intrigue treated the work of art as a container for something altogether mysterious and absolutely unknowable even to him, enticing the beholder to test the object and introducing sound into the work of art.[25]

After becoming familiar with Duchamp's art, Johns continued to invite participation. For example, his casts of everyday objects, such as a flashlight or ale can, solicit the touch needed to activate them; however, the viewer would be surprised to discover their great weight and artificiality. The spectator might also be shocked by his suddenly intimate relationship with the work of art, handling it in this way.[26] In certain paintings of the late 1950s and early 1960s, by the inclusion of actual objects such as rulers and sticks, Johns acknowledged the observer and his space, as well as induced his reach.[27]

With the recognition that art ought not, in fact, be handled, Johns often in the mid 1960s, provoked perceptual participation. Viewers are presented with pairs of maps, flags and ale cans, whose differences seem to welcome discernment, and compositions that trigger after images. Such visual stimulation and enticement of the beholder continued in the 1970s, with the crosshatch patterns, in which one might discover systems at work in the seemingly random marks, and in the 1970s and 1980s, with the numerous images that contain more than one identity.[28]

Perhaps Duchamp's most ambitious participatory work was revealed at the Philadelphia Museum of Art in 1969: *Etant Donnés: 1° la chute d'eau, 2° le gaz d'éclairage*. The visitor finds himself in a small, empty, unlit room, where, if somewhat inquisitive, he notices a large, old Spanish door at one end. With further daring, the intrepid individual discovers, in this frontal, two-dimensional 'image', a pair of peep holes; these demonstrate that *Etant Donnés* is a container which, nevertheless, allows for

Fig. 5 *Decoy*, 1971

perceptual entry. Upon looking in, the unwary visitor observes a provocative, even shocking, tableau, and may at once realize some embarrassment at the position in which he now finds himself.

Not long after *Etant Donnés* was revealed in Philadelphia, Johns made *Decoy*, 1971 (fig. 5). Here, a single gromet near the bottom edge can serve as a kind of peep hole. But recognizing the limitations on his objects to be literally acted upon, and accepting a synthetic approach to the problem of inviting or depicting viewer involvement, Johns shows in the middle of the canvas what could be imagined as behind the canvas but viewable through the hole. In an appropriately dark and dramatic setting to isolate the object which has, like Duchamp's tableau, been indiscreetly discovered, an ale can is revealed. It makes a perfect anti-climax, because having seen through one wall 'into' the work of art, the viewer will be frustrated to find yet another container,

Fig. 6 *Voice 2*, 1971

one that withholds its contents until opened and consumed.[29] Above this penultimate container, Johns wrote: FRONT OF ALE CAN, thus indicating that the spectator can go no further, that an ultimate, perhaps inviolable space exists which remains unavailable. Having extended the borders of his work of art, and urged the participation of the 'watchman', Johns has laughingly turned him away with but a 'Decoy'.[30]

Sound was a major component of Johns's earliest attempts to expand the boundaries of art. It is a part of *Construction with Toy Piano*, about which Johns explained 'I was interested in the idea of a painting that did more than one thing, that had another aspect. That was the reason for the sound.'[31] *Tango* had the same capacity,[32] as did *Target with Plaster Casts*, which, initially, he intended to have been 'a sort of piano' that would produce noises when the keys were touched.[33] The addition of sound and touch to the visual work gave the possibility of a synesthetic effect. Johns planned, too, for the viewer's thoughts and expectations, as well as his physical movement toward the object, thereby adding yet more sensory perceptions to this complex experience of art.

Because Johns had to accommodate the fact that visual art could not usually be handled, he became comfortable with the notion of a conceptual or figurative inclusion of sound instead of a literal one. In *Voice 2*, 1971 (fig. 6), his use of the title word is ingenious. By separating its letters into three sections, he coaxed viewers to articulate the sounds, thereby forming the whole word, and at the same time activating the object itself.[34] With this strategy, Johns brings sound to the work of art, even though the object itself is not capable of producing it on its own.

A similar scheme may be at work in a series of images that focuses on an outstretched arm to recall the suicidal death by drowning of the poet Hart Crane.[35] Upon seeing the first four letters emphasized in the word YELLOW, viewers are encouraged to speak the word yell, which describes the sound that occurred when Crane was seen jumping over the railing of a ship.[36] Adding to this pattern of articulated, desperate sounds is *Painting Bitten By a Man*, 1961 (Collection of the artist). By having bitten into the paint, Johns formed a mark that not only shows the action of his open mouth, but the sound that could have been made simultaneously. This effect suggests that his interest in Edvard Munch may have begun long before usually acknowledged;[37] if one thinks of the Norwegian's print *The Scream*, the comparison is striking: Munch depicted a sound that radiates in space and that even seems to have the potential to be heard by viewers, and Johns has made a literal analogue of that scream.

During the 1970s and 1980s, Johns continued to explore the possible ways of invoking or suggesting sound as part of a two-dimensional art work. For instance, he uses titles to invest a canvas figuratively with the sounds of a lament, in *Weeping Women*, 1975 (Newhouse Collection, New York), or the chirping of an insect, in *Cicada*, 1979 (pl. 2). But in a watercolour, also titled *Cicada*, 1979 (pl. 1), he adds a drawing of the insect in the lower register to show the source of the imagined sound. The combination of the crosshatch pattern with the predella section, such as one finds in medieval altarpieces, approximates the kind of juxtaposition that is seen in *Target with Plaster Casts*. These juxtapositions parallel the musical practice of counterpoint, although in *Cicada*, it is a particularly dissonant example, for the maudlin collection of skulls, insects, and messages at the bottom is a jarring contrast with the serene image above.

Continuing to create artificial situations in which sound is suggested or pretended, Johns shows the open mouth of a whale in *Ventriloquist*, 1983 (The Museum of Fine Arts, Houston), inviting the viewer to strain his ears to hear the sounds that might emanate from the animal.[38] The title can be interpreted as a joke about the depicted situation, since if the whale is the dummy, the ventriloquist must be the artist hiding behind the painted surface. It is his 'voice' we, paradoxically, see, not hear, in beholding the painting. If we strain further, we might even hear the sounds of running water that Johns has so frequently painted during the 1980s.[39] In the altogether magical *Perilous Night*, 1982 (pl. 14), Johns literally alludes to music and sound by including the sheet music for a work by John Cage. This music is, of course, as real as that found earlier in *Tango*, although ironically it is an example of music that is silent. Still, Cage's notations welcome the musically adept to read and sing the notes, thereby bringing sound to the visual work.[40]

Johns has always been a great reader, especially of poetry, and solver of crossword puzzles, hence words fascinate him and occupy an important position in his art. At first, following so many others,[41] he embedded newsprint in his encaustic paintings of the 1950s. This inclusion allowed for the introduction of ideas, events, feelings, and all kinds of content, even if the emotions involved were not his own.[42] But out of this exercise came the possibility of a painting that could be read, which was a perverse and outrageous insult for formalist-minded individuals of the 1950s, but which Johns pursued anyway and emphasized in such works as *The Book* (Margulies Collection, Miami), and *The Newspaper* (Lee Collection, New York), both of 1957.

While Johns's earliest inclusions of words were for subordinate purposes, their assimilation had been accomplished, and he soon realized other possibilities. Enlarged to state 'Tango', the type had a much more emphatic presence, and the potential to allude to something beyond the object, to music, dance, an era, and a mood. In *False Start* (fig. 7), of 1959, he introduced a situation in which the words RED, YELLOW, BLUE seem to lie if seen only in the context of the painting; the words do not accord with the painted colours over which they appear nor even the colours with which they are delineated.

Speaking recently about the subject of writing, Johns noted that this activity results in the explanation of 'a feeling'. He continued: 'Words are interesting. Painting isn't words, so you know that using words would mean making something else.'[43] Yet that

Fig. 7 *False Start*, 1959

Fig. 8 *Periscope (Hart Crane)*, 1963

is what Johns has done. Even as he recognizes in this passage the potential use of words and then discounts that usage in painting, he has, nevertheless, explored language in his imagery. This contradiction suggests that his comment was intended ironically, and that he is, in fact, involved in 'making something else'.

Just as in poetry, Johns has explored the potential for similarly short expressions to suggest a great deal. For example, his use of the word *Tango* has this quality, and his naming *Tennyson* at the bottom of a painting of 1958 (Des Moines Art Center) went further in the same evocative spirit. While specific inclusions of poetry are almost nonexistent in Johns's work,[44] he may have been seeking an allusive sense by naming the primary colours in *Periscope (Hart Crane)*, 1963 (fig. 8). The pairing of the small RED lying perspectively behind the larger one, and the opposite rendering of BLUE(s) suggests a kind of echo effect, but the voice is still somehow in control of itself. The YELLOW, by contrast, is tumultuous and out of control. Do the words themselves mean anything in this situation? Certainly nothing to do with colour designations, it would appear. But perhaps given the context of a suicidal event, Johns used the words for a fragmentarily poetic effect: red (alert), yell, blue (mood). Hence, his words, too, 'explain a feeling', and give the painted object a new direction in which to move.[45]

Johns's most cautiously approached inclusion was himself and his emotions. Early in his career, he preferred that art not be an 'exposure' of his feelings;[46] but a better statement of his intentions might have been the occasion on which he said that at that period he preferred to 'hide my personality, my psychological state, my emotions'.[47] 'Hide' is the more accurate word because it suggests that what is missing is not so far away, perhaps behind or somehow within the art object. But how might he have been masking himself in the early work? In effect, the flags and maps identify the maker as an American; the numbers and rulers indicate an individual fond of calculating and measuring; Tennyson suggests a reader of poetry; the body parts are the outer aspects of an individual's physique; the Savarin can full of paint brushes is the attribute of a painter; and the Ballantine cans belong to someone who likes his ale. What we have then is a public persona contained inside these art works, hidden in the subject matter that has been selected.

Fig. 9 *In Memory of My Feelings – Frank O'Hara*, 1961

Fig. 10 *Study for Skin 1*, 1962

In the early 1960s, Johns broached his more vulnerable side, in works such as *In Memory of My Feelings — Frank O'Hara*, 1961 (fig. 9). Just by naming his friend's poem, Johns called forth his own emotional self. A good deal more of his feelings were contained, or perhaps buried is a better term, beneath the paint in the upper right corner. X-rays show that Johns originally included an image of a skull with the words DEAD MAN in that section.[48] This may have been the first occasion in which he used that vanitas symbol, although at about the same time, he wrote in his notes: 'A Dead Man/ Take a skull/Cover it with paint. Rub it/against canvas. Skull against/ canvas.'[49] During the following year, Johns let himself and his 'psychological state' show through the two-dimensional surface, from behind, in *Study for Skin 1* (fig. 10). Although seen through a kind of veil, his emotional pose recalls that of the terrified figure in *The Scream* by Munch. In 1964, Johns created the already discussed *Souvenir 2*, which diagrams his relationship to the picture plane and how a work of art contains him. In this exposed position, he presents himself with a far more impassive visage.

Johns's next advance in including an individual within the art object was a cluster of related works, the *Tantric Detail* and *Dancers on a Plane* series (pls. 7-10 and 3-6), in which the subjects are not, however, identifiable with him. In the former group of images, he exhibits fragments of a person — a skull and testicles — 'plastered' onto a crosshatch pattern. These works are a culmination of ideas that appear in 1960-61, for we have seen that the first indication of a skull in Johns's paintings dates to 1961; and in 1960, he made *Painting with Two Balls* (Collection of the artist), which anticipates the overt appearance of testicles in the *Tantric* pictures. Choosing just these characteristics as the sole indicators of a human presence, Johns makes the twin themes of death and eros the most evocative aspects of the human condition.

More playful is the related series of paintings, each entitled *Dancers on a Plane* (pls. 3-6). Johns's title is a witty incongruity that likens the activities of dancers and painters, each of whom is known for their movements on a flat surface. The title also draws attention to a contrast with Johns's earlier work, namely, the figure now resides *on* the plane, not behind, within, integrated with or imagined there as before. In the last decade and a half, Johns has increasingly applied human presences 'on a plane',[50] rather than integrated with or behind the canvas.

The two large paintings titled *Dancers on a Plane*, dating 1979 and 1980, form a fascinating pair. Like the two *Cicada* works, there is an impression that one is a seamless image, perhaps of an exterior self, whereas the second is darker and more melancholy, as if the interior view has come forward or is being seen through the surface, as was the case in the *Skin* series. It is tempting, too, to consider the pair as parts of a diptych, such as Johns's *Corpse and Mirror*, of 1974 (Ganz Collection, New York), wherein a model reality on the left (comparable to the 1979 *Dancers*) is juxtaposed with an altogether flawed reaction to it, or inside out version, on the right.

The earlier *Dancers on a Plane* consists of a pattern of crosshatchings on one side mirrored across a vertical, division line on the other. Reading from the top down, there are three horizontal divisions, at which the clusters of primary-coloured lines cross but change direction or colour, or both. The marks at the left and right edges of the canvas can, it is imagined, be joined to form a cylindrical composition, like the skin of a human torso. If there is a dancer here, the figure is suggested by this device and by the words of the title, the letters of which are interspersed with the artist's name and date of the work. The painting, then, is the idea or analogue of a dancer. In 1980, perhaps encouraged by his work on the *Tantric* series, Johns more forcefully conveyed the sense of a figure.

Johns introduces testicles at the top edge of the 1980 *Dancers* and a vagina at the bottom to suggest copulation such as is seen in Tantric imagery.[51] The colours have become blotted and clotted, as if an indication of an imprecise yet moody characterization. With half of the lettering reversed, unlike the 1979 painting, Johns suggests that we are viewing both sides of one work of art, or perhaps its contents. Although the pattern of hatch marks is the same as in the earlier painting, Johns does not show the mirror arrangement of colours across the vertical division. Now, there are pictorial events that are unaccounted for, which is all quite human and to be expected if one is looking beyond the outer appearance of a container to its inner workings.

Framing the sides of each painting is a sequence of applied knives, forks, and spoons that in its regular rhythm complements the subtleties of the crosshatch patterns and creates a sense of that counterpoint discussed earlier. Johns had used these implements in a number of works, but here they might be seen as epitomizing an audience observing and 'consuming' the performance of the dancers.[52] The juxtaposition of two worlds, that of the audience and that of the performer (the former occupying a real space, the latter a plane), recalls Johns's frequent emphasis on the observer's position in relation to the work of art.

The *Dancers on a Plane* series is another instance of Johns combining various art forms – dance, visual art, language, and perhaps music in the form of the polyphonic composition – in a single image. It might be surmised that he even has an ambition to create a kind of Gesamtkunstwerk, with visual art being just the start of a larger, synesthetic experience. But most notable for this study is his evolving effort toward including a human depiction on the picture plane, in this case by a series of clues. Johns's effort has a comic coda, for in *Usuyuki (Study for Merce Cunningham Minnesota Residency Poster)*, of the following year (pl. 11), all it takes to accomplish this goal is to use words.

Johns would continue to imply a human presence within his crosshatch patterns in such masterful works as *Between the Clock and the Bed* (pls. 12 and 13). Here, he employs the title to suggest that something or someone is caught between the two and that in fact the painting is an abstraction of a representational idea. The title is borrowed from a work by Munch of the same name, thereby further reinforcing the interpretation that Johns's patterns refer to a narrative. With these cues, it is not difficult for the viewer to imagine an abstracted figure trapped within the crosshatch webbing in the middle of the canvas.

For the artist conventionally described as the precursor of Pop art, it is especially curious to discover that other, recurring inclusions in Johns's work are passages of purely abstract painting. Perhaps the first instance of this occurred in 1957, when he depicted an American flag on a painterly, orange field of colour, literally a 'Flag on a Plane' not unlike a dancer on a plane. About this work, Johns said that he wanted 'to have more than one element in the painting and . . . to be able to extend the space beyond the limits of the image'. [53] In other words, as with the nearly contemporary *Target with Plaster Casts*, he again emphasized two kinds of space, one of which belongs to the flat field of the canvas and one that is characteristic of life.

Between 1963 and 1965, Johns continually composed bars, circles, and blocks of colour with recognizable subjects.[54] As in the 1957 *Flag on Orange Field* (Museum Ludwig, Cologne), he forced the viewer to note similarities and differences between diverse entities on the same canvas. On one level, these juxtapositions may have a disjointed character, for example, in *Map*, of 1963 (Private collection, New York), the ostensibly meaningless primary colours, in blocks along the right edge, contrast dramatically with the associations implied by a map of the United States. But one also observes that the colour rectangles are similar to the regular shapes of some states; might the former have been intended to gain associations of the latter just by this juxtaposition? As with Johns's explorations of language, context is all-important in influencing apparent meaning.

The shape of such areas of colour and their regular arrangement often have a similarity to the contemporaneous colour slabs of Hans Hofmann. This likeness was as much 'ready-made' as many others of Johns's appropriated subjects, that, as with a flag or some bit of newsprint, there are pre-existing associations in a quote of a celebrated formalist painter.[55] Johns returned to this theme in the 1980s, with depictions of a print by Barnett Newman that he owned.[56] Unlike Hofmann, who abstained from directing the viewer toward an intended meaning, Newman claimed a specific significance for his abstract imagery. Newman's is not an approach that Johns would take, but by referring to him or suggesting Hofmann-like fragments within his own canvases, Johns compared divergent approaches in art. Perhaps most telling, the abstract passages of his predecessors' paintings are inherently self-revealing, whereas each of Johns's canvases is a container for extensive, sometimes unseen, contents.

Should Johns's various machinations perhaps be termed stratagems as the title of this study suggests? Like a spider that weaves a maze to catch the unwary, recalling Bernardo Bertolucci's film title *The Spider's Stratagem*, Johns seems to strategize specifically for the purpose of playing with, deceiving, and ultimately outwitting the history of art, historians, critics, and viewers alike. Think once more of his parable of the 'spy' and the 'watchman'. Though they both need each other for the work of art to succeed, Johns, the spy, constantly exploits the watchman's expectations, to such an extent that the latter becomes a kind of opponent. In this mental combat, the puzzle-like character of a work of art can never be thoroughly unravelled, for each object is a container with only its outer shell and fragments of its interior contents visible. Indeed, perhaps most unknowable of all in its fullest dimension is the emotional aspect of Johns's work that lies simmering beneath the surface. While barely hinted at, these feelings are among the driving forces in his art.

Mark Rosenthal

I am grateful to Jasper Johns for commenting on my manuscript, and to George Marcus for editing it.

1   For more on this subject, see Jasper Johns's comments in Walter Hopps, 'An Interview with Jasper Johns', *Artforum*, vol. 3, no. 6 (March 1965), pp. 35-36.

2   Quoted in David Sylvester, 'Interview', in Arts Council of Great Britain, London, *Jasper Johns Drawings* (Museum of Modern Art, Oxford, 17 September-13 October, 1974), p. 17.

3   Quoted in Michael Crichton, *Jasper Johns* (New York, 1977), p. 34.

4   See Roberta Bernstein, 'An Interview with Jasper Johns', in *Fragments: Incompletion & Discontinuity*, ed. Lawrence D. Kritzman (New York, 1981), pp. 279-90.

5   'The question of what is a part and what is a whole is a very interesting problem, on the infantile level, yes, on the psychological level, but also in ordinary, objective space.' Quoted in Peter Fuller, 'Jasper Johns Interviewed: Part II', vol. 18 (September 1978), p. 56. Consider, as well, the following statement by Johns: 'An object that tells of the loss, destruction, disappearance of objects. Does not speak of itself. Tells of others. Will it include them? Deluge.' Quoted in New York, The Jewish Museum, *Jasper Johns* (16 February-12 April, 1964), p. 22. And: 'Whether to see the 2 parts as one thing or as 2 things.' Quoted in Jasper Johns, 'Sketchbook Notes', *0 to 9*, no. 6 (July 1969), p. 2.

6   Quoted in Sylvester, 'Interview', p. 10.

7   See Fuller, 'Johns Interviewed: II', p. 7.

8   See, also, *Untitled*, c. 1954 (Hirshhorn Museum), and *Star*, 1954 (Private collection, Los Angeles).

9   See Johns's statement in Sylvester, 'Interview', p. 9.

10 *Ibid*, pp. 9, 16, 18.

11 For example, *Scent*, 1974 (Ludwig Collection, Aachen).

12 For example, the *Dancers on a Plane* series discussed and illustrated in this study.

13 See Johns's comments quoted in Joseph E. Young, 'Jasper Johns: An Appraisal', *Art International*, vol. 13, no. 7 (September 1969), p. 51.

14 *Ibid*.

15 'The watchman falls "into" the "trap" of looking. The "spy" is a different person. "Looking" is and is not "eating" and "being eaten." (Cezanne? – each object reflecting the other.) That is, there is continuity of some sort among the watchman, the space, the objects. The spy must be ready to "move", must be aware of his entrances and exits. The watchman leaves his job & takes away no information. The spy must remember and must remember himself and his remembering. The spy designs himself to be overlooked. The watchman "serves" as a warning. Will the spy and the watchman ever meet? In a painting named SPY, will he be present? The spy stations himself to observe the watchman. If the spy is a foreign object, why is the eye not irritated? Is he invisible? When the spy irritates, we try to remove him. "Not spying, just looking" – Watchman.' Quoted in Jasper Johns, 'Sketchbook Notes', *Art and Literature*, vol. 4 (Spring 1965), p. 185.

16 Johns makes 'puns on intentions', to use his words, in this work and in *Untitled*, c. 1954 (Hirshhorn Museum). By collaging foreign newsprint (that is 'foreign bodies'), he suggests the unconventional, additive nature of his enterprise. Regarding the 'puns', see Jasper Johns, 'Sketchbook Notes', *Julliard* (1968-69), pp. 25-27; reprinted in Richard Francis, *Jasper Johns* (New York, 1984), p. 110.

17 Bernstein, 'An Interview', p. 287.

18 *Ibid.*

19 See Roberta Bernstein, *Jasper Johns' Paintings and Sculptures 1954-1974* (Ann Arbor, 1985), p. 34.

20 Among other aspects of this relationship, Johns's choice of flags and numbers as subject matter shows a consciousness of the idea of the 'readymade', in the spirit of Duchamp's found objects.

21 Jasper Johns, 'Thoughts on Duchamp', *Art in America*, vol. 57, no. 4 (July-August, 1969), p. 31.

22 Jasper Johns, 'Marcel Duchamp (1887-1968): An Appreciation', *Artforum*, vol. 7, no. 3 (November, 1968), p. 6.

23 *Ibid.*

24 See, for example, *Bicycle Wheel*, 1913, for the involvement of the sense of touch, and for movement of the art work; *Bell Alain* and *Belle Haleine*, 1921, for the sense of smell; *Prière Toucher (Please Touch)*, 1947, for the sense of touch, and for the viewer theoretically being enticed into a sexual encounter. See, also, *Why Not Sneeze Rrose Sélavy*, 1921, and *With Hidden Noise*, 1916, in both of which the writing beneath the objects can only be viewed by actual handling or with a mirror. See Bernstein, *Paintings and Sculptures*, pp. 60-68, for additional information regarding the relationship of Johns to Duchamp.

25 See also Duchamp's 50cc of Paris Air (Air de Paris), in which the art work contains something that is invisible.

26 In *Field Painting*, 1963-64 (Private collection), a button invites the viewer's attention.

27 Among others, *Painting with Two Balls*, 1960 (Collection of the artist); *Device Circle*, 1959 (Tremaine Collection, New York); *4 the News*, 1961 (Kunstsammlung Nordrhein-Westfalen, Düsseldorf); *Zone*, 1962 (Kunsthaus, Zurich).

28 There are also numerous double and tromp l'oeil images to fool the eye in this period.

29 Johns describes the work of art as being eaten in the aforementioned discussion of the 'spy' (note 15). For further discussion of the point, see Mark Rosenthal, *Jasper Johns, Work Since 1974* (Philadelphia, 1988), pp. 44, 46.

30 For additional discussion of the relationship of the beholder to Johns's work, see Michael Crichton, 'The Function of the Observer', *Johns*, pp. 73-99.

31 Quoted in *ibid*, p. 65, n. 5.

32 At first, Johns employed in *Tango* a music box which played 'Silent Night', but very soon after altered it so that unidentifiable sounds would be emitted (interview with author, September 1989).

33 Bernstein, 'An interview', p. 287.

34 A similar strategy occurs in each version of *Racing Thoughts* (1983 and 1984, The Whitney Museum of American Art and Robert and Jane Meyerhoff

Collection, Phoenix, Maryland, respectively). Along the left edge, one discovers that GLACE/WARE (or glassware) can be articulated within a German language sign.

35 For example, *Land's End*, 1963 (San Francisco Museum of Modern Art); *Diver* (Braman, 1962 Collection, Miami Beach); and *Passage*, 1962 (Museum Ludwig, Cologne).

36 The effect of YELL in YELLOW was noted by Bernstein, *Paintings and Sculptures*, pp. 109-10.

37 The relationship of Johns to Munch was first mentioned with regard to the *Between the Clock and the Bed* series, 1981-83, by Francis, *Johns*, p. 100.

38 One also notes an open-mouthed duck in *Spring*, 1986 (Newhouse Collection, New York).

39 See Johns's various untitled works of 1983-84, illustrated in Rosenthal, *Johns*, and the discussion of the faucet in the same source, p. 72.

40 One can also interpret the sheet music as a parallel to the systems that Johns employs to carry out his crosshatch compositions; that is, sheet music is a plan for a performance.

41 For example the Cubists, Kurt Schwitters, Joseph Cornell and Robert Rauschenberg, all of whom embedded newsprint in their works.

42 Johns has often denied that there were any specific meanings intended by him in his choices of newsprint (Hopps, 'Interview', p. 33).

43 Ann Hindry, 'Conversation with Jasper Johns', *Art Studio*, no. 12 (Spring, 1989), p. 8.

44 One exception is *Skin with O'Hara Poem*, 1963-65 (lithograph).

45 Bernstein emphasizes Johns's interest in the sonnets of Ted Berrigan, and notes that he was especially interested in the following line by the poet: 'Everything turns into writing/I strain to gather my absurdities into a symbol', from *Sonnets* (New York, 1967), p. XLV. Bernstein, *Paintings and Sculptures*, p. 132.

46 Crichton, *Johns*, p. 20.

47 Peter Fuller, 'Jasper Johns Interviewed: Part I', *Art Monthly*, vol. 18 (July-August 1978), p. 7.

48 I thank Stefan Edlis and Gael Neeson for kindly sharing these X-rays with me.

49 Quoted in Jewish Museum, *Johns*, p. 26.

50 For example, the figurative fragments in *Untitled*, 1972 (Museum Ludwig, Cologne); the footprint in *Fizzles*, 1975-76 (etchings); handprints in *Céline*, 1978 (Kunstmuseum, Basel); and the shadow figures in the various versions (painted and etched) of the *Seasons*.

51 Conversation with the author, September 1989.

52 For further discussion of this point, see Rosenthal, *Johns*, pp. 44-47. Also, the combination of two fields of existence is comparable to Degas's views of an

orchestra pit together with the performers above, images which Johns finds of interest (conversation with the author, 1988).

53 Quoted in Hopps, 'Interview', p. 35.

54 For example, *Map*, 1963 (Private collection, New York); *Arrive/Depart*, 1963-64 (Bayerische Staatsgemalde-sammlungen, Munich); *According to What*, 1964 (Newhouse Collection, New York); *Watchman*, 1964 (Hiroshi Teshigahara, Tokyo); *Untitled*, 1964-65 (Stedelijk Museum, Amsterdam); and *Eddingsville*, 1965 (Museum Ludwig, Cologne).

55 One is tempted to make much more of Johns's citations of Hofmann, in as much as the latter was a darling of Clement Greenberg, the esteemed formalist critic who was not so fond of Johns. Hofmann might have become a symbol of the past generation, not only for Johns but for Rauschenberg, who also made extensive use of Hofmann-like colour slabs, especially in the early 1960s. While similarly rectilinear planes of colour occur often in the 20th century (in the works of Kandinsky, Schwitters, Malevich, Chagall, and Duchamp, for example), Hofmann's blocks of colour were being painted in the same period that Johns and Rauschenberg were utilizing the forms. Is it but an accident, then, that in the middle of Johns's *Usuyuki*, 1977-78 (Collection of the artist), one discovers a newsprint line: *Hofmann's right arm creased?*

56 The Newman lithograph appears in the aforementioned *Ventriloquist*, and reversed in *Racing Thoughts*. Johns was friendly with Newman and tells the story that on one occasion of their meeting, Newman informed him that he had considered titling his recently completed series entitled *Who's Afraid of Red, Yellow and Blue*, 1969-70, instead, *Who's Afraid of Jasper Johns* (conversation with the author, 1988).

Details of Figures

Fig 1 *Target with Plaster Casts*, 1955, Encaustic and collage on canvas with plaster casts in wood construction, 51 × 44 × 3½ inches (Collection Mr. Leo Castelli).

Fig 2 *Souvenir 2*, 1964, Oil and collage on canvas with objects, 28¾ × 21 inches (Collection Mrs. Victor W. Ganz).

Fig 3 *Construction with Toy Piano*, 1954, Graphite and collage with toy piano, 11 × 9 × 2 inches (Collection Kunstmuseum Basel).

Fig 4 *Tango*, 1955, Encaustic on canvas with music box, 43 × 55 inches (Private collection, Germany).

Fig 5 *Decoy*, 1971, Oil on canvas with object, 72 × 50 inches (Collection Mrs. Victor W. Ganz).

Fig 6 *Voice 2*, 1971, Oil and collage on canvas, 72 × 50 inches each panel, 3 panels (Collection Kunstmuseum Basel).

Fig 7 *False Start*, 1959, Oil on canvas, 67¼ × 54 inches (Collection Mr. and Mrs. S. I. Newhouse, Jr.).

Fig 8 *Periscope (Hart Crane)*, 1963, Oil on canvas, 67 × 48 inches (Collection of the artist).

Fig 9 *In Memory of My Feelings – Frank O'Hara*, 1961, Oil on canvas with objects, 40 × 60 inches, 2 panels (Collection Stefan T. Edlis).

Fig 10 *Study for Skin 1*, 1962, Charcoal on drafting paper, 22 × 34 inches (Collection of the artist).

WORKS IN THE EXHIBITION

JOHN CAGE

Solo for Piano

from Concert for Piano and Orchestra

1957-58

Ink on paper 63 pages, each $11 \times 16\frac{7}{8}$ inches

with additional title page and explanatory notes

Northwestern University Music Library, John Cage 'Notations' Collection

MERCE CUNNINGHAM

Videos

STORY

1964, 20 minutes, black and white

Choreography by Merce Cunningham. Directed by Hakki Seppala. Music by Toshi Ichiyanagi: *Sapporo*. Set and Costumes by Robert Rauschenberg. Produced by the Finnish Broadcasting Company.

VARIATIONS V

1966, 50 minutes, black and white

Choreographed by Merce Cunningham. Directed by Arne Arnbom. Music by John Cage *Variations V*. Distortion of television images by Nam June Paik. Film images by Stan VanDerBeek. Produced by Studio Hamburg. Norddeutscher Rundfunk.

WALKAROUND TIME

1973, 48 minutes, colour

Choreography by Merce Cunningham. Directed by Charles Atlas. Music and soundtrack by David Behrman: '. . . *for nearly an hour* . . .'. Decor supervised by Jasper Johns based on Marcel Duchamp's *The Large Glass*, in the Philadelphia Museum of Art.

EVENT FOR TELEVISION
1977, 56 minutes, colour

Choreography by Merce Cunningham. Directed by Merrill Brockway. Music by John Cage: *Branches (For Amplified Plant Music)*; and by David Tudor: *RainForest (An Electronic Ecology)*. Produced by Emile Ardolino.

MERCE BY MERCE BY PAIK
1978, 45 minutes, colour

Part I: *Blue Studio* (1976), 15 minutes, colour. Choreography by Merce Cunningham. Directed by Charles Atlas and Merce Cunningham. Produced at WNET/TV Lab.
Part II: *Merce and Marcel* (1978), 30 minutes, colour. By Nam June Paik and Shigeko Kubota. Sound score: David Held, Earl Howard and John Cage.

LOCALE
1980, 30 minutes, colour

Choreography by Merce Cunningham. Directed by Charles Atlas. Music by Takehisa Kosugi: *Interspersion*. Design by Charles Atlas. Produced by Cunningham Dance Foundation.

MERCE CUNNINGHAM
1980, 60 minutes, colour

A documentary directed by Geoff Dunlop. Produced by The South Bank Show, London Weekend Television.

CHANNELS/INSERTS
1982, 32 minutes, colour

Choreography by Merce Cunningham. Directed by Charles Atlas. Music by David Tudor: *Phonemes*. Artistic Adviser: Mark Lancaster. Produced by Cunningham Dance Foundation.

SOMETIMES IT WORKS, SOMETIMES IT DOESN'T
1983, 63 minutes, colour

Directed by Chris Dercon and Stefaan Decostere. Produced by Belgian Radio & Television.

POINTS IN SPACE
1986, 55 minutes, colour

Choreography by Merce Cunningham. Directed by Elliot Caplan and Merce Cunningham. Music by John Cage : *Voiceless Essay*. Set by Bill Anastasi. Costumes by Dove Bradshaw. Produced by Bob Lockyer (BBC TV) and Cunningham Dance Foundation.

CHANGING STEPS
1989, 35 minutes and 18 seconds, colour

Choreography by Merce Cunningham. Directed by Elliot Caplan and Merce Cunningham. Music by John Cage : *Cartridge Music* (1960) recorded at Théâtre de la Ville, Paris, December 1988. Design by Elliot Caplan. Costumes by Mark Lancaster and Suzanne Gallo. Produced by Cunningham Dance Foundation and La SEPT.

JASPER JOHNS

1

Cicada

1979

Watercolour and pencil on paper

$38\frac{1}{2} \times 28$ inches

Collection of the artist

2

Cicada

1979

Oil on canvas

$30\frac{1}{2} \times 22$ inches

Private collection

140

3

Dancers on a Plane

1979

Oil on canvas with objects

$77\frac{7}{8} \times 64$ inches

Collection of the artist

4

Dancers on a Plane

1980

Oil on canvas with painted bronze frame and objects

$78\frac{3}{8} \times 63\frac{3}{4}$ inches

The Trustees of the Tate Gallery

5

Dancers on a Plane

1980-81

Oil on canvas

$29\frac{7}{8} \times 23\frac{3}{4}$ inches

Private collection

6

Dancers on a Plane

1982

Graphite on paper

35×27 inches

Collection of the artist

7

Tantric Detail

1980

Charcoal on paper

58×41 inches

Collection of the artist

8

Tantric Detail I

1980

Oil on canvas

$50\frac{1}{8} \times 34\frac{1}{8}$ inches

Collection of the artist

9

Tantric Detail II

1981

Oil on canvas

$50\frac{1}{8} \times 34\frac{1}{8}$ inches

Collection of the artist

10

Tantric Detail III

1981

Oil on canvas

$50\frac{1}{8} \times 34\frac{1}{8}$ inches

Collection of the artist

11

Usuyuki (Study for Merce Cunningham Minneapolis Residency Poster)

1981

Ink, watercolour and lithography on plastic

$36\frac{1}{4} \times 57$ inches

Robert and Jane Meyerhoff, Phoenix, Maryland

12

Between the Clock and the Bed

1981

Watercolour and pencil on paper

$22\frac{1}{4} \times 31$ inches

Collection of the artist

13

Between the Clock and the Bed

1981

Oil on canvas

$72 \times 126\frac{1}{4}$ inches

Collection of the artist

14

Perilous Night

1982

Ink on plastic

$31\frac{5}{8} \times 40\frac{7}{8}$ inches

The Art Institute of Chicago

through prior gift of Mary and Leigh Block;

Harold L. Stuart Endowment

CHRONOLOGIES

John Cage preparing a piano, before 1950

JOHN CAGE

1912

Born September 5, in Los Angeles, the only son of the engineer and inventor John Milton Cage, and his wife Lucretia Harvey.

1920-28

Takes piano lessons from his Aunt Phoebe and Fannie Charles Dillon. Becomes fascinated by the piano music of Edvard Grieg.

1927

Representing Los Angeles High School, wins Southern California Oratorical Contest with his speech *Other People Think*, a plea for Pan-American conscience on the part of American people, their government and industry.

1928

Graduates from Los Angeles High School; class valedictorian. Enters Pomona College where he remains for two years. Is attracted to the writing of Gertrude Stein.

1930-31

Travels to Europe, spending six months in Paris studying architecture with Goldfinger, and piano briefly with Lazare Levy. Moves on to Biskra, Majorca, Madrid and Berlin, writing poetry and painting. Begins to compose music.

1931-34

Returning to the USA, continues to write, paint, and compose; gives lectures on music and art to housewives. Studies composition with pianist Richard Buhlig in Los Angeles. Develops method of chromatic composition dealing with the problem of keeping repetitions of individual tones of a twenty-five tone range as far as possible, even though each voice expresses all twenty-five tones before introducing a repetition of any one of them. Studies with Adolph Weiss and Henry Cowell in New York.

1934-35

Studies counterpoint and analysis with Arnold Schönberg privately, at the University of Southern California, and at UCLA. Promises Schönberg to devote his life to music. Marries Xenia Andreyevna Kashevaroff.

1936

Through association with the film-maker Oscar von Fischinger becomes interested in noises, and subsequently, because of little feeling for harmony, develops methods of writing percussion music and rhythmic structure for it.

1937

Joins modern dance group at UCLA as accompanist and composer. Studies bookbinding with Hazel Dreis; forms quartet of bookbinders for playing of percussion music.

1938

Moves to Seattle as composer-accompanist for Bonnie Bird's modern dance classes at the Cornish School. Meets Merce Cunningham, then a student of Bonnie Bird, and the artists Mark Tobey and Morris Graves. Composes and performs percussion music for a group which he organizes and tours throughout the Northwest. Collects instruments of many kinds including 'junk' objects. Delivers lecture entitled 'The Future of Music: Credo' in which he defines music as 'organization of sound'. Summer: on faculty and works as composer for Marian Van Tuyl, Mills College, California. Fall: composes music for *Bacchanale* (dance by Syvilla Fort), the first prepared piano piece.

1939

Composes *Imaginary Landscape No. 1* using muted piano, cymbal and phonograph records of variable and constant frequencies played on turntables having variable speed and requiring the use of a recording studio for its performance. Moves to San Francisco, gives concerts of percussion music with Lou Harrison. Employed as a recreational leader for the Works Progress Administration.

1940

Spends year trying unsuccessfully to establish a centre for experimental music with university or corporate support.

1941

At invitation of László Moholy-Nagy, teaches a class in experimental music at the Chicago School of Design. Commissioned by CBS to write scores for Kenneth Patchen's Columbia Workshop radio play *The City Wears a Slouch Hat*. Accompanies dance classes of Katherine Manning.

Moves to New York City in the spring, and writes *Credo in Us*, his first work to accompany a dance by Merce Cunningham and the beginning of a lifelong collaboration. Writes *The Wonderful Widow of Eighteen Springs* for Janet Fairbanks (his first use of a text from James Joyce's *Finnegan's Wake*) to be accompanied by fingers or knuckles striking the lid of a closed grand piano. Meets Marcel Duchamp through Max Ernst and Peggy Guggenheim.

1943

Concert of percussion music under his direction at the Museum of Modern Art in February begins to establish his reputation as a central figure of the avant-garde. Meets Virgil Thomson, who becomes a friend and supporter of his work.

1944

Cage becomes closely associated with Cunningham with their first joint recital. From the mid-1940s to the present often writes music for and performs with Cunningham, and their invention of the independent but cooperative relationship of music and dance has a profound effect on others.

1945-47

Separated from Xenia, moves to the Lower East Side. Begins to study the philosophy and classical music of India with Gita Sarabhai, and attends lectures on the philosophy of Zen Buddhism by Dr. Daisetz T. Suzuki at Columbia University (for two years). Tours with Merce Cunningham.

1947

The Ballet Society of New York commissions his score for *The Seasons*, with choreography by Cunningham and decor by Isamu Noguchi. Writes music for Duchamp sequence in Hans Richter's film *Dreams That Money Can Buy*.

1948

Completes *Sonatas and Interludes* for prepared piano, to express the nine permanent emotions of Indian aesthetics, having read works by Ananda K. Coomaraswamy. Teaches during the summer at Black Mountain College in North Carolina, where he presents an Erik Satie Festival. Meets R. Buckminster Fuller, whose thought will become increasingly important for him.

1949

Receives Guggenheim Fellowship and an award from the American Academy and National Institute of Arts and Letters. Travels to Europe, where he meets Pierre Boulez,

with whom he later carries on a lively correspondence. Gives concerts and dance recitals in Paris with Cunningham. Continues his studies of Satie, bringing back to New York the unpublished *Vexations* and three pieces of the *Furniture Music*.

1950

Meets the pianist David Tudor, with whom he collaborates on many performances and projects over the following years. Together with Tudor and the composers Morton Feldman, Christian Wolff, and (somewhat later) Earle Brown, works to free sounds from memory, taste, and any fixed relationship to each other. Over the next few years they make constant experiments and discoveries in the field of music for magnetic tape. Delivers *Lecture on Nothing* and *Lecture on Something* at the Artists Club started by Robert Motherwell in New York. During this period, becomes a friend of many of the Abstract Expressionist painters, who constitute a sympathetic audience to his music and Cunningham's dance.

1951

Completes *Sixteen Dances* for Cunningham, for which he prepares charts to determine the note to note procedure of the music. Wolff introduces Cage to the *I Ching* (Chinese Book of Changes) which becomes an essential tool for composing much of his music and, later, his texts and prints. Over a period of nine months, writes *Music of Changes* for piano, based entirely on chance operations. New Music Society commissions *Imaginary Landscape No. 4* for twelve radios. Receives first prize at the Woodstock Film Festival for his music for Herbert Matter's film *Works of Calder*.

1952

Teaches again at Black Mountain College, where he organises an untitled event with Cunningham, Robert Rauschenberg, Tudor, and the poets Charles Olson and Mary Caroline Richards. This 45 minute event, in which each participant simultaneously performs unrelated actions, is later seen as a prototpye for the 'Happenings' of the mid 1960s. During summer also works on *Williams Mix*, a complex piece for tape using a large number of recorded sounds spliced together in chance determined ways. Collaborates with Robert Rauschenberg on *Automobile Tire Print*. Writes *4′33″*, a silent piece in three movements, encouraged by Rauschenberg's white canvases, one of which hangs in his appartment.

1953

Formation of Merce Cunningham Dance Company with Cage as Musical Director.

1954

Moves with David Tudor, Mary Caroline Richards, David and Karen Weinrib to a small cooperative community founded by Paul and Vera Williams near Stony Point, New York, where he becomes fascinated with the study of mushrooms in particular and nature in general. Makes a European concert tour with David Tudor which has a lively effect upon experimental music abroad. Meets Jasper Johns.

1955

Writing *Music for Piano* by noticing imperfections in the paper he is using. Gives controversial recital with Cunningham's Company in October at the Clarkstown High School in New City, New York.

1956

Gives occasional classes (through 1960) at the New School for Social Research in New York, where his students include George Brecht, Al Hansen, Dick Higgins, Toshi Ichiyanagi, Allan Kaprow, and Jackson Mac Low. Later developments in Happenings and the Fluxus movement partly attributed to his teaching.

1958

In May, a retrospective concert of 25 years of Cage's music is organized by Johns, Rauschenberg, and Emile de Antonio at Town Hall in New York. *Concert for Piano and Orchestra*, with a piano solo using 84 different kinds of composition is performed for the first time, David Tudor playing the piano part, Merce Cunningham conducting as a 'chronometer of variable speed'. A group of Cage's original scores is shown at the Stable Gallery. With David Tudor, travels to Europe, giving three lectures on 'Composition as Process' in Darmstadt, where he meets Nam June Paik. At Brussels World Fair delivers lecture 'Indeterminacy, New Aspect of Form in Instrumental and Electronic Music', consisting of 30 stories read one each minute. At the invitation of Luciano Berio, spends four months in Milan, composing *Fontana Mix* with notations on transparent plastic, different realisations of which may be made. Wins Italian TV quiz show 'Lascia O Radoppia' as mushroom expert, and on the same show performs *Water Walk* and *Sounds of Venice*, two short audio-visual works.

1959-60

Virgil Thomson, a book on the composer and critic, in collaboration with Kathleen Hoover, is published by Yoseloff, New York. Teaches courses at the New School for Social Research in mushroom administration, experimental composition, and the music of Virgil Thomson.

1960-61

Fellow at Center for Advanced Studies at Wesleyan University, Middletown, Connecticut, where he works on *Silence*, first anthology of his lectures and writings, published by Wesleyan in 1961. Shifts his interest with David Tudor from music for magnetic tape to live electronic music. Writes *Cartridge Music* for phonograph cartridges and contact microphones to pick up small sounds, and uses materials from the score to write other music and texts, including *Where Are We Going And What Are We Doing?* Completes flexible text on Rauschenberg, published in May 1961. Commissioned by the Montreal Festival Society to write a major orchestral work, *Atlas Eclipticalis*, composed with astronomical charts and *I Ching* chance operations.

1962

Co-founds the New York Mycological Society with Lois Long, Esther Dam, Guy G. Nearing and Ralph Ferrara. Travels to Japan on six week concert tour with David Tudor.

1963

In September, organizes and presents first New York performance of Satie's *Vexations*, with 840 repetitions. Writes *Variations III and IV*, indeterminate works for any number of performers, any sound producing means.

1964

Writes *26 Statements re Duchamp* and completes *Jasper Johns: Stories and Ideas* for Johns exhibition at the Jewish Museum. New York Philharmonic Orchestra, at the instigation of Leonard Bernstein, performs *Atlas Eclipticalis* with mixed reaction from audience and orchestra. In April, invited by University of Hawaii music department to visit as Western part of an East-West meeting, Toru Takemitsu representing the East. Travels with Cunningham Company on world tour which includes Thailand, Japan and India.

1965

Begins writing intermittent text *Diary: How to Improve the World (You Will Only Make Matters Worse)* to celebrate the ideas of R. Buckminster Fuller. Becomes President of the Cunningham Dance Foundation and a Director of the Foundation for Contemporary Performance Arts. New York Philharmonic commissions *Variations V*, danced by Merce Cunningham.

1966

Variations VII premieres during Nine Evenings sponsored by Experiments in Art and Technology, Inc.

1967

Composer in residence at University of Cincinnati. Finishes second anthology of writings, *A Year From Monday*, published by Wesleyan in 1968. Introduced to Henry David Thoreau's *Journal* by the poet Wendell Barry. Organizes first *Musicircus* at University of Illinois, Urbana, in November, consisting of simultaneous performances of as many unrelated musics as obtainable and practical in the given time and space.

1968

Conceives *Reunion*, a plurality of continuously activated sound systems gated by moves on an electronically prepared chess board, performed in Toronto with Marcel and Teeny Duchamp, David Behrman, Lowell Cross, Gordon Mumma, and David Tudor. Elected to the American Academy and Institute of Arts and Letters.

1968-69

Awarded Thorne Music Scholarship. An Associate at the Center for Advanced Study at the University of Illinois in Urbana, collaborates with Lejaren Hiller on work for harpsichords and tapes, dividing the octave in all ways from 5 to 56 tones. For this project computer facilities and sound output are utilised. *HPSCHD* is performed in the Assembly Hall at Urbana on 16 May 1969, with 7 harpsichords, 51 tapes, 7 film projectors and 80 slide projectors for an audience of 9,000. Many of the slides and films are on the subject of space travel.

1969

Artist in residence, University of California at Davis. Publishes collection of scores assembled for the Foundation for Contemporary Performance Art as *Notations* (with Alison Knowles, New York : Something Else Press). Executes first major graphic work, *Not Wanting to Say Anything About Marcel*, with Calvin Sumsion. Begins work on *Cheap Imitation*, derived from Satie's *Socrate*, by chance operations, for piano, and later for orchestra, and violin. Increasingly interested in working with language, to free it from syntax and fixed meaning.

1970

Again appointed Fellow for Advanced Studies at Wesleyan University. Makes increasing use of Thoreau's writing to derive both music and prose. Writes *Song Books* for solo voices referring (and not referring) to the theme 'We connect Satie with Thoreau'. Praeger publishes the anthology *John Cage*, edited by Richard Kostelanetz. Writes *36 Acrostics re and not re Marcel Duchamp*.

1971

Letrasets 62 *Mesostics re Merce Cunningham*, subjecting over 700 type faces and sizes to chance operations. Studies the writings of Mao Tse-tung. Exhibition of Cage's work at Galleria Schwarz, Milan.

1972

Produces *Mushroom Book* (with Lois Long and Alexander H. Smith), for which he makes 10 handwritten lithographs. European concert tour with David Tudor, often performing *Mesostics* or *Mureau* (mix of Thoreau's remarks about sound and music) superimposed on Tudor's eletronic works. Around this time, moves back to Manhattan from Stony Point.

1973

A selection of scores and plexigrams shown at Carl Solway Gallery, Cincinnati. *M* is published by Wesleyan University.

1974

Begins extended work for solo piano, *Etudes Australes*, again using star charts. Thinking of the right and left hands as independent of one another, discovers that a single hand can play circa 640 different 4-note aggregates and about the same number of different 5-note aggregates. Employs Thoreau's drawings for musical composition in *Score with Parts*. Contributes *Series re Morris Graves* to catalogue of the artist's drawings.

1975

Exploring ways to encourage improvisation while avoiding memory and taste, writes *Child of Tree* for amplified plant materials. Commissioned by Canadian Broadcasting Corporation for a work related to the Bicentennial of the USA : *Lecture on the Weather* combining twelve collages of spoken Thoreau texts with film of Luis Frangella and breeze, rain, and thunder recordings by Maryanne Amacher.

1976

Commissioned by Seiji Ozawa and the Boston Symphony Orchestra for a major Bicentennial work, writes *Renga* (using 361 Thoreau drawings) and *Apartment House 1776*, incorporating live or recorded songs, Sephardic, Protestant, Slave and American Indian. Intensive preoccupation with *Finnegan's Wake* begins.

1977

Advised by Yoko Ono to consult Shizuko Yamamoto, adopts macrobiotic diet. Score for *Renga* exhibited at the Museum of Modern Art, New York. Begins to write *Freeman Etudes* for violinist Paul Zukofsky in precisely determinate notation. Continues improvisational research with music of contingency, a music in which there is a break in the connection between cause and effect, writes *Inlets* for conch shells filled with water and then tipped to allow for gurgles.

1978

At the invitation of Kathan Brown, begins sessions of printmaking at Crown Point Press in Oakland, California, using chance operations and experimenting with various techniques. Crown Point publishes *Score without Parts (40 Drawings by Thoreau): Twelve Haiku, Seven Day Diary (Not Knowing), 17 Drawings by Thoreau* and *Signals* (36 related etchings). Makes *Sounday* for KRO in Amsterdam, ten uninterrupted hours of radio broadcast, *Il Treno* for the Teatro Communale in Bologna, three variations on a theme by Tito Gotti, trains prepared with the assistance of Juan Hidalgo and Walter Marchetti. Publishes *Writing through Finnegans Wake* (with Alison Knowles). Elected a Fellow of the American Academy of Arts and Sciences. Groups of scores and etchings shown at Carl Solway Gallery, New York, at Museum Folkwang, Essen, Städtische Museum, Mönchengladbach and Kunstverein, Cologne, and also at San Francisco Art Institute, Atholl McBean Gallery.

1979

At IRCAM in Paris, assisted by sound engineer John Fullemann, commissioned by West German Radio, Dutch Catholic Radio, and South German Radio, produces *Roaratorio, an Irish Circus on Finnegan's Wake*, using several thousand sounds mentioned in the *Wake* or recorded in place, referred to in it by Joyce. Devises a means of 'translating' any book into music. Receives Carl Sczuka Prize for *Roaratorio*. Gives first night long performance of *Empty Words* in the course of a Festival of his work in Bonn. Selection of scores and publications shown at Kunstforum, Bonn. *Writing Through Finnegan's Wake* is published by Printed Editions, New York. *Empty Words* is published by Wesleyan.

1979-80

Changes and Disappearances, an unfinished etching project, is published by Crown Point Press.

1980

Completes *Third* and *Fourth Writings through Finnegan's Wake*. Begins *Fifth Writing*. Completes *James Joyce, Marcel Duchamp, Erik Satie: An Alphabet*. Selection of scores and etchings shown at Boston College Gallery, Newton, Massachusetts. Elected University of California Regents Lecturer, San Diego.

1981

In September, gives night long performance of *Empty Words* broadcast over National Public Radio from Real Art Ways in Hartford, Connecticut, where his scores and etchings are being exhibited. Presents *Composition in Retrospect*, referring to his own past works, at the eighth Computer Music Conference in Denton, Texas, in November. In the same month, *Thirty Pieces for Five Orchestras* is given its premiere in Pont-a-Mousson, near Metz, France. Begins *Dance/4 Orchestras* for the Cabrillo Music Festival in 1982. *For the Birds*, conversations with Daniel Charles, is published by Marion Boyars, Salem, New Hampshire. *Another Song*, with photographs by Susan Barron, is published by Calloway Editions, New York.

1982

Completes two extended sequences of prints at Crown Point Press, *Changes and Disappearances* and *On the Surface*, and begins and completes another series, *Dereau*. *Roaratorio* is performed both in Toronto at the end of January and later in May in London. 'Wall-to-Wall Cage and Friends' is presented at Symphony Space in New York in March. Bowery Ensemble presents ten hours of his music at Cooper Union early in April. Whitney Museum of American Art exhibits Cage's scores and prints. *Themes and Variations* is published by Station Hill Press, Barrytown, New York. The *Mud Book*, made with illustrations by Lois Long in the late 1950s, is published in facsimile by Callaway Editions. The Witten Festival in West Germany, a festival at the Theater am Turm in Frankfurt, the Pro Musica Nova in Bremen for which he plans *A House Full of Music*, a circus of unprofessional music involving 800 schoolchildren, the 10th New Music Festival in Tokyo, Mayor Byrne's New Music America in Chicago, celebrations at the Walker Art Center in Minneapolis for which he writes *Postcard from Heaven* for 1–20 harps and at the American Center in Paris are all dedicated to Cage in view of his 70th birthday. Composes *Fifteen Domestic Minutes* for National Public Radio, September 5, bringing performances in Los Angeles, Denver, New York City and Washington, D.C. into a single broadcast by means of satellite transmission. One man exhibitions at Albright-Knox Art Gallery, Buffalo, New York; Philadelphia Museum of Art; Museum of Contemporary Art, Chicago; Margarete Roeder Fine Art, New York. Etchings shown at Crown Point Press. Awarded the Commandeur de l'Ordre des Arts et des Lettres, France.

1983

Receives the Notable Achievement award from Brandeis University. *Roaratorio* performed in Lille, France and Frankfurt, West Germany with special choreography by Merce Cunningham and the participation of the Merce

Cunningham Dance Company. Teaches at the International Summer-academy in Viitasaari (Finland). Inducted into the Percussive Arts Society Hall of Fame. Creates *Weathered I–XII* , a series of colour photographs realized by Paul Barton and begins *Where R = Ryoanji* (drawings and etchings).

1984

Begins 'work in progress' *Music For ――* (title completed by number of parts performed). HMCIEX produced in Cologne and broadcast by KUSC in Los Angeles as part of the Olympic Arts Festival contemporary Music Program. Begins to work with IBM PC (assisted by Andrew Culver and Jim Rosenberg) and writes the first computer assisted mesostic, *Writings Through Howl* (after the poem by Allen Ginsberg). One man exhibitions at the Fruitmarket Gallery, Edinburgh and at Galleriet Anders Tornberg, Lund, Sweden.

1985

Exhibition of scores and drawings at Kölnischer Kunstverein, Cologne. Work at Crown Point Press: *Fire*, series of 16 monotypes, *Ryoku*, series of 13 prints, *Mesostics: Earth, Air, Fire, Water*, 12 collage monoprints, and *HV (horizontal-vertical)*, 36 monotypes. Jim Rosenberg begins programme for a mesostic intelligent word processor. *A Collection of Rocks* premiers at the XII Music Biennale in Zagreb, Yugoslavia. *Music for Nine* at São Paulo Biennale. Begins work on *Europeras 1 & 2* commissioned by the Städtische Bühnen in Frankfurt. Writes *The First Meeting of the Satie Society*. With the help of computer analysis, begins *Essay*, a synthesis of various readings of *Writings Through the Essay: On the Duty of Civil Disobedience* by Henry David Thoreau. *John Cage and Merce Cunningham*, an exhibition at Margarete Roeder Fine Art.

1986

At Crown Point Press: *Eninka*, series of 50 monoprints. Finishes *Essay*. Receives degree Doctor of All the Arts Honoris Causa from California Institute of the Arts. Makes *The First Meeting of the Satie Society* accessible electronically on the Art Com Electronic Network carried by the WELL (Whole Earth 'Lectronic Link) through Telenet. Rosenberg finishes mesostic processor. *Etcetera 2/4 Orchestras* premiered as part of the Suntory International Program for Music Composition in Tokyo. First simultaneous performance of all the *Ryoanji* versions at the New Music America Festival in Houston. Selection of work shown at Galerie Watari, Tokyo. One man exhibition at Blum Helman Gallery, New York.

1987

Work at Crown Point Press: *Where There is Where There*, a series of 38 related images, *Deka*, series of 35 related images, and *Variations*, series of 35 monotypes. Twenty-four continuous hours of live radio broadcast at WDR in Cologne are devoted exclusively to his works (February 14 and 15). Dokumenta 8 in Kassel presents *Essay*, 18 different readings by Cage over 36 loudspeakers, as a sound-installation. The Los Angeles Festival dedicates a full week of concerts and events to John Cage on the occasion of his 75th birthday. December premiere of *Europeras 1 & 2*, at the Schauspielhaus Theatre of the Städtische Bühnen, after fire in Frankfurt Opera house delays November opening. 'NACHTCAGETAG' exhibition, West German Radio, Cologne.

1988

Travels to Leningrad as guest of the Moscow Union of Composers of the USSR. USA premiere of Frankfurt Opera production of *Europeras 1 & 2*, at Pepsico Summerfare. At the instigation of Ray Kass, executes a series of 52 paintings, the *New River Watercolors*, at the Miles C. Horton Center at the Virginia Polytechnic Institute and State University. The paintings begin a tour of several Virginia museums and will be shown at the Phillips Collection in Washington D.C. in 1990. As the Charles Eliot Norton Professor of Poetry for the 1988-89 academic year, Cage gives a series of 6 lectures and 6 seminars at Harvard University, to be published by The Harvard University Press. Elected to the World Academy of Arts and Sciences. *Where There is Where There* is shown at the University Art Museum, Berkeley, California.

1989

Charles Eliot Norton lectures and seminars continue. Work at Crown Point Press: *Nine Stones* and *Nine Stones 2, Ten Stones* and *Ten Stones 2, Eleven Stones* and *Eleven Stones 2, Empty Fire, Urban Landscape* (alteration of *Where There is Where There*), *Global Village 1 - 36* and *Global Village 37 - 48*. First performance of *Seven*, co-commissioned by Boston Musica Viva and Voices of Change. The Boston Symphony Orchestra and the Fromm Music Foundation at Harvard University commission *101*, for first performance at Symphony Hall in Boston on 6 April. Cunningham Dance Foundation produces gala event to 'Celebrate Cage'. Cage begins working again on the *Freeman Etudes* for solo violin, numbers XVII–XXXII. Inducted into the American Academy and Institute of Arts and Letters. Becomes a laureate of the Kyoto Prize 1989 given by the Inamori Foundation.

MERCE CUNNINGHAM

1919

Born Mercier Cunningham, 16 April, in Centralia, Washington, second son of Clifford D. and Marion Cunningham.

c. 1929

First dance lessons with a local teacher.

c. 1932

Begins to study tap and ballroom dancing with Maude M. Barrett.

c. 1935

Tours west coast with Mrs Barrett and her daughter, Marjorie.

1936-1937

On graduation from High School, attends George Washington University, Washington, DC, for one year.

1937

Enrols at Cornish School, Seattle, Washington, as drama student. Studies modern dance with Bonnie Bird and transfers to Cornish dance department.

1938

Attends Summer School at Mills College, Oakland, California. Dances with Bella Lewitzky in *Conquest* by Lester Horton. Meets John Cage, who is engaged as dance accompanist at Cornish in the fall. Cage teaches dance composition classes in which he encourages students to write music for their own dances. Cunningham plays in Cage's percussion concerts. Meets Morris Graves and Mark Tobey. First student choreographies.

1939

Attends Bennington College School of Dance summer session at Mills College, Oakland, California. Dances in 'Men's Dance' from Doris Humphrey's *New Dance*, choreographed by Charles Weidman. Invited by Martha Graham to join her company. Leaves Cornish and travels to New York, arriving in September. First performances with Martha Graham Dance Company, New York, December: Acrobat in *Every Soul is a Circus*.

1940

Creates roles of Christ Figure in *El Penitente* and March in *Letter to the World*. Begins to study at School of American Ballet.

1941

Creates role of Pegasus in *Punch and the Judy*.
Moves into loft at 12 East 17 Street, New York.

1942

During Graham company summer residency at Bennington, gives joint concert with Jean Erdman and Nina Fonaroff: programme includes *Seeds of Brightness* (music by Norman Lloyd), *Credo in Us* (John Cage, text by Cunningham), and *Ad Lib* (Gregory Tucker), all choreographed and danced in collaboration with Jean Erdman, and a solo, *Renaissance Testimonials* (Maxwell Powers); repeat performances in October in New York, with a new solo, *Totem Ancestor* (Cage).

1943

Performs in John Cage's percussion concert at Museum of Modern Art, New York. Performs with Erdman at Arts Club of Chicago, repeating duets and adding two new solos with music by Cage: *In the Name of the Holocaust* and *Shimmera*. Choreographs and dances in *The Wind Remains*, a zarzuela after Lorca by Paul Bowles, at Museum of Modern Art. Creates role of Poetic Beloved in Graham's *Deaths and Entrances*.

1944

First solo concert with John Cage: six solos with music by Cage: *Triple-Paced*, *Root of an Unfocus*, *Tossed As It Is Untroubled*, *The Unavailable Memory of*, *Totem Ancestor*, *Spontaneous Earth*. Music and dance composed to a common time structure, coming together at main structural points but otherwise independent. *Four Walls*, a dance play with text and choreography by Cunningham, music by Cage, designed by Arch Lauterer, performed at Perry-Mansfield Workshop, Steamboat Springs, Colorado; cast includes Julie Harris and Cunningham. Creates role of Revivalist in Graham's *Appalachian Spring*. Choreographs *Idyllic Song* (Erik Satie).

1945

Second New York solo concert; programme includes *Mysterious Adventure* (Cage), with costume and object after a design by David Hare, and *Experiences* (Cage and Livingston Gearhart). Leaves Graham company.

1946

Third New York concert: three new solos: *The Encounter* (Cage), *Invocation to Vahakn* (Alan Hovhaness), *Fast Blues* (Baby Dodds drum improvisation), and a trio, *The Princess Zondilda and her Entourage* (Alexei Haieff, text by Cunningham).

1947

Ballet Society commissions *The Seasons*, with music by Cage, designs by Isamu Noguchi. Cunningham dances leading role with Tanaquil LeClercq and other members of Balanchine's Ballet Society company. Fourth New York concert: *The Open Road*, solo with music by Lou Harrison; *Dromenon* (Cage) for Cunningham and six women.

1948

First tour of the United States by Cunningham and Cage, including first visit to Black Mountain College, North Carolina. New solo, *Dream* (John Cage). Cunningham and Cage invited to spend summer at Black Mountain. Cage arranges Satie Festival, ending with performance of *The Ruse of Medusa*, translated by M. C. Richards. Directed by Arthur Penn, scenery by Willem and Elaine de Kooning, properties by Richard Lippold, Ray Johnson et al. Cast includes Cunningham, Buckminster Fuller, Elaine de Kooning. Cunningham gives concert including *The Monkey Dances* from *The Ruse of Medusa*; a new solo, *Orestes* (Cage); and trio, *A Diversion* (Cage). Teaches modern dance at School of American Ballet.

1949

The Seasons included in inaugural season of New York City Ballet. Second tour of United States. Cunningham and Cage leave for Europe; give concerts in Jean Hélion's studios and at Théâtre de Vieux Colombier with Tanaquil LeClercq and Betty Nichols of Ballet Society company. Programme includes trio, *Effusions avant l'heure* (Cage) and duet, *Amores* (Cage), with LeClercq. Article, 'An American in Paris', published in November *Dance Observer*. Solo, *Two Step* (Satie).

1950

Fifth New York concert: new quartet, *Pool of Darkness* (music by Ben Weber), and new solo, *Before Dawn* (in silence). David Tudor works with Cunningham for first time. Choreographs two works for Louisiana State University Dance Group: *Waltz* (Satie) and *Rag-Time Parade* (Satie). Solo version of *Waltz* (Satie). In the fall, again teaches modern dance at School of American Ballet (until spring of 1951).

1951

Sixteen Dances for Soloist and Company of Three (Cage/Remy Charlip et al). First use of chance processes, to determine sequence of dances and in actual choreography of final quartet. Cage and Cunningham tour Western states: in Denver, Colorado, they meet Carolyn and Earle Brown. *Variation* (Morton Feldman), chance solo using ballet steps. 'The Function of a Technique for Dance' published in *The Dance Has Many Faces*, edited by Walter Sorell.

1952

Invited by Leonard Bernstein to choreograph two works for Festival of the Creative Arts at Brandeis University, Waltham, Massachusetts: *Les Noces* (Stravinsky) and excerpts from *Symphonie pour un homme seul* (Pierre Schaeffer and Pierre Henry). Choreographs two versions of Schaeffer's *musique concrète* work, a solo and a group of dance, using chance processes, with gamuts of everyday movements, social dance steps, and phrases choreographed by Cunningham; dance and music are totally independent of one another, simply occupying the same length of time. Summer at Black Mountain; performs in Cage's Theatre Piece. 'Space, Time and Dance' published in *trans/formation* Volume I, No 3. Carolyn and Earle Brown move to New York.

1953

Merce Cunningham and Company perform at University of Illinois, Urbana: *Suite by Chance* (Christian Wolff/Remy Charlip). *Solo Suite in Space and Time* (Cage), choreographed according to a chance process based on imperfections in a sheet of paper (as was Cage's music). Summer residency at Black Mountain with his dancers, including Brown, Viola Farber, Marianne Preger, Remy Charlip, and Paul Taylor. Session ends with two performances with programs including *Banjo* (Louis Moreau Gottschalk), *Septet* (Erik Satie), *Dime a Dance* (19th century piano music arranged by David Tudor), all with costumes by Remy Charlip, and *Untitled Solo* (Christian Wolff). Cunningham decides to keep the company together and to give a New York season at the end of the year at Theater de Lys. Repertory augmented by *Amores* and *Trio* (formerly *Games*), *Suite by Chance* in its entirety, and a new group dance, *Fragments* (Pierre Boulez/Charlip).

1954

First Guggenheim Fellowship for choreography. *Minutiae* (John Cage), first collaboration with Robert Rauschenberg.

1955

Springweather and People (music by Earle Brown/design by Remy Charlip, Rauschenberg, Ray Johnson, Vera Williams). *The Young Disciple*, a play by Paul Goodman, directed and designed by Julian Beck, dances by Cunningham, presented at Living Theater, New York. First U.S. tour by Merce Cunningham Dance Company. Nicola Cernovich becomes lighting designer. 'The Impermanent Art' published in 7 *Arts* No. 3.

1956

Galaxy, 'a quartet of solos' for Brown, Farber, Preger, Charlip (music by Earle Brown/costumes by Charlip); *Lavish Escapade*, solo for Cunningham (Christian Wolff/ costume by Cunningham); *Suite for Five* (Cage/ Rauschenberg); *Nocturnes* (Erik Satie/Rauschenberg).

1957

Labyrinthian Dances (Josef Matthias Hauer/Rauschenberg); *Changeling*, solo (Christian Wolff/Rauschenberg); *Picnic Polka*, a companion piece to *Banjo* (Louis Moreau Gottschalk/Charlip); revised version of *Springweather and People*, with new designs by Rauschenberg.

1958

Cunningham conducts first performance of Concert for Piano and Orchestra at John Cage retrospective concert at Town Hall, New York. *Suite for Two* (duet version of *Suite for Five*, with new solo for Brown, 'A Meander') and *Collage I* (later called *Collage III*), new solo for Cunningham. First summer residency at Connecticut College School of the Dance, New London, with performances at Eleventh American Dance Festival; *Antic Meet* (Cage/Rauschenberg) and *Summerspace* (Morton Feldman/Rauschenberg). Cunningham, Cage, Brown, and Tudor perform in Stockholm, Brussels, and Hamburg; *Night Wandering* (music by Bo Nilsson/costumes by Nicola Cernovich – later redesigned by Rauschenberg).

1959

From the Poems of White Stone (Chou Wen-Chung/ Rauschenberg) and *Gambit for Dancers and Orchestra* (Ben Johnston/Rauschenberg) commissioned by University of Illinois. Second Guggenheim Fellowship. *The Cave at Machpelah* by Paul Goodman, directed and designed by Julian Beck, dances by Cunningham, presented by Living Theater. Second summer at New London: *Rune* (Christian Wolff/Rauschenberg). Merce Cunningham Studio opens in Living Theater building, 6th Avenue and 14th Street, New York.

1960

Rauschenberg, Jasper Johns, and Emile de Antonio present performance by Dance Company at Phoenix Theater, New York. Cunningham and Brown perform in second Cage *Theatre Piece* at Composer's Showcase concert, New York. *Dance* Magazine award. Third summer at New London: *Crises* (Conlon Nancarrow/Rauschenberg). Cunningham, Cage, Brown, and Tudor again tour in Europe; performances in Venice, Berlin, Munich, Cologne, and Brussels. Repertory includes two new solos for Carolyn Brown: *Hands Birds* (Earle Brown/Rauschenberg) and *Waka* (Toshi Ichiyanagi/Rauschenberg), and *Music Walk with Dancers* (Cage/Rauschenberg). Robert Dunn begins to teach composition courses at Merce Cunningham Studio, out of which comes Judson Dance Theater.

1961

Suite de danses, choreographed for Canadian television (Serge Garrant/Johns). Fourth summer at New London. *Aeon* (Cage/Rauschenberg) performed at Festivals de Montréal. Rauschenberg begins to travel with company as lighting designer and technical director.

1962

The Construction of Boston, directed by Cunningham, with text by Kenneth Koch, design by Rauschenberg, Jean Tinguely, Niki de Saint-Phalle, presented at Maidman Theater, New York.

1963

Summer residency at University of California, Los Angeles: *Field Dances* (Cage/Rauschenberg) and *Story* (Toshi Ichiyanagi/Rauschenberg), both indeterminate pieces.

1964

Paired (Cage/Rauschenberg); *Winterbranch* (La Monte Young/Rauschenberg). Formation of Cunningham Dance Foundation. Six-month world tour with performances in Strasbourg, Paris, Bourges; Venice, Vienna, Mannheim, Essen, Cologne, les Baux de Provence; Dartington Hall, Devon; London, where one week at Sadler's Wells is followed by three weeks at Phoenix Theater; Stockholm; Turku and Helsinki (Finlandl); Prague and Ostrava (Czechoslovakia); Warsaw and Poznan (Poland); Krefeld, Brussels, Antwerp, Scheveningen; Bombay, Ahmedabad, Chandigarh, New Delhi; Bangkok; Tokyo, Kobe, and Osaka. At Museum des 20. Jahrhunderts, Vienna, company performs Museum Event No. 1. *Cross Currents* (Nancarrow arr. Cage). Cunningham receives Medal from Society for Advancement of Dancing in Sweden. Rauschenberg leaves company at end of tour. Cunningham moves to apartment on Mulberry Street.

Merce Cunningham with notes for *Canfield*, 1969

1965

Variations V (Cage/film by Stan VanDerBeek). *How to Pass, Kick, Fall and Run* (Cage: stories).

1966

Summerspace staged for New York City Ballet. Merce Cunningham Studio moves to 498 Third Avenue; Cunningham also moves to this address. 'Summerspace Story' by Merce Cunningham published in *Dance* Magazine. Company begins to make yearly tours abroad. *Place* (Gordon Mumma/Beverly Emmons). *Variations V* filmed for West German television. Gold Medal for Choreographic Inventions at 4th International Festival of Dance, Paris.

1967

Cunningham and Cage tour New York State College campuses in 'Contemporary Voices in the Arts' (with Robert Creeley, Billy Klüver, Len Lye, Jack Tworkov, and Stan VanDerBeek). Jasper Johns appointed Artistic Adviser. *Scramble* (Ichiyanagi/Frank Stella). North German Television film, *498 Third Avenue*. *Summerspace* revived for Cullberg Ballet, Stockholm.

1968

RainForest (David Tudor/Andy Warhol); Walkaround Time (David Behrman/design supervised by Jasper Johns, based on Marcel Duchamp's *The Large Glass*). Company becomes resident company at Brooklyn Academy of Music. Jasper Johns designs 'target' poster. 'An Appetite for Motion,' profile of Cunningham by Calvin Tomkins, published in *The New Yorker* (reprinted in *The Bride and the Bachelors*). Central-South American tour. Frank Stella designs poster for tour. *Changes: Notes on Choreography*, edited by Frances Starr, published by Something Else Press, New York. Filming of *Assemblage* for KQED-TV, San Francisco.

1969

Canfield (Pauline Oliveros/Robert Morris). Robert Rauschenberg designs poster for BAM season.

1970

Tread (Christian Wolff/Bruce Nauman); *Second Hand* (Cage/Johns); *Signals* (Cage-Mumma-Tudor); *Objects* (Alvin Lucier/Neil Jenney). 'Choreography and the Dance', interview with Cunningham, published in *The Creative Experience*, edited by Stanley Rosner and Laurence E. Abt (New York: Grossman Publications).

1971

Studio moves to Westbeth Artists' Housing complex; Cunningham and Cage move to apartment on Bank Street. *Loops*, solo event at Museum of Modern Art, in front of Jasper Johns's 'Map' (Gordon Mumma/slides by Charles Atlas).

1972

Landrover (Cage-Mumma-Tudor/Johns); *TV Rerun* (Mumma/Johns); *Borst Park* (Christian Wolff). Receives Brandeis University Creative Arts Award Medal. Honorary Degree of Doctor of Letters, University of Illinois. *Canfield* wins Grand Prix, International Theatre Festival, Belgrade. Carolyn Brown leaves company. Charles Atlas films *Walkaround Time* in Brooklyn and Paris. 'Dance: East and West' by Merce Cunningham published in *Essays on Asian Theater and Dance* (New York: Performing Arts Program of the Asia Society).

1973

Changing Steps (Cage/Mark Lancaster). *Un jour ou deux* (Cage/Johns) commissioned by Festival d'automne for Paris Opéra Ballet.

1974

'Diaghilev/Cunningham' exhibition at Emily Lowe Gallery, Hofstra University, Hempstead, Long Island. 'A Video Event', two-part television programme taped for CBS Camera Three, directed by Merrill Brockway. *Westbeth* (Cage/Mark Lancaster), first work for video by Cunningham and Atlas, taped at Merce Cunningham Studio. *Summerspace* and *Winterbranch* revived by Boston Ballet.

1975

Exercise Piece (Lancaster); *Rebus* (David Behrman/Lancaster); *Sounddance* (Tudor/Lancaster); *Solo* (Cage/Sonja Sekula). New York State Award. *Merce Cunningham*, photographs by James Klosty, with contributions by Klosty, Carolyn Brown, Viola Farber, Lewis L. Lloyd, John Cage, Robert Rauschenberg, Jasper Johns, et al; published by Saturday Review Press, New York. Portfolio of seven prints recording collaborations with Merce Cunningham and Dance Company, by John Cage, Jasper Johns, Robert Morris, Bruce Nauman, Robert Rauschenberg, Frank Stella, and Andy Warhol, with text by Calvin Tomkins and photographs by James Klosty, published by Multiples Inc. and Castelli Graphics. *Blue Studio: Five Segments*, solo videodance, directed by Charles Atlas, taped at WNET/TV Lab, New York.

1976

Torse (Maryanne Amacher/Lancaster); *Squaregame* (Takehisa Kosugi/Lancaster). *Squaregame Video*, directed by Atlas, taped at Merce Cunningham Studio. *Summerspace* revived by Théâtre du Silence, La Rochelle, France. 'Event for Television', taped for WNET's 'Dance in America' series, directed by Merrill Brockway; includes *Video Triangle* (Tudor/Lancaster).

1977

First Broadway season, Minskoff Theater, New York: *Travelogue* (Cage/Rauschenberg). Exhibition of Cunningham's Notes and Notations on Dance, Carl Solway Gallery, New York. Capezio Award. Dual screen filming of *Torse*, directed by Atlas. *Inlets* (Cage/Morris Graves); Seattle residency poster by Morris Graves. Washington State Award. *Fractions* (Jon Gibson/Lancaster), directed by Atlas, taped at Westbeth.

1978

Stage version of *Fractions*. Exercise *Piece I*; *Exercise Piece II* (Cage/Lancaster). First season at City Center Theater, New York: *Exchange* (Tudor/Johns); *Tango*, solo (Cage/Lancaster). *Exchange* filmed at University of California, Berkeley. Cunningham and Cage move to apartment on West 18th Street.

1979

Locale (Kosugi/design and direction Atlas) filmed at Merce Cunningham Studio. *Changing Steps* revived by Théâtre du Silence, Paris. American Dance Guild Award. *Roadrunners* (Yasunao Tone/Lancaster) commissioned by American Dance Festival. 'Merce Cunningham', documentary by Geoff Dunlop for South Bank Show. Stage version of *Locale*.

1980

Mark Lancaster appointed Artistic Adviser. Second City Center season: *Duets* (Cage/Lancaster); *Exercise Piece III* (Cage/Lancaster). *Fielding Sixes* (Cage/Monika Fullemann). *Le Danseur et la Dance*, entretiens avec Jacqueline Lesschaeve, published by Pierre Belfond, Paris.

1981

Channels/Inserts (Tudor/design and direction Atlas), filmed at Merce Cunningham Studio. *Signals* revived by the Ohio Ballet. Third City Center season, New York: *10's with Shoes* (Martin Kalve/Lancaster); stage version of *Channels/Inserts*. Poster by Jasper Johns for residency at Walker Art Center, Minneapolis. *Gallopade* (Kosugi/Lancaster). Cunningham Cage, and Chris Komar conduct International Dance Course for Professional Choreographers and Composers, University of Surrey, Guildford.

1982

Fourth City Center season: *Trails* (Cage/Lancaster). *Duets* revived by American Ballet Theater. 'A Collaborative Process Between Music and Dance' by Merce Cunningham published in *TriQuarterly 54*, Spring. Merce Cunningham receives Samuel H. Scripps American Dance Festival Award. *Quartet* (Tudor/Lancaster). *Merce Cunningham and Company*, documentary by Benoit Jacquot, produced by l'Institut National de l'Audiovisuel and Cunningham Dance Foundation. Merce Cunningham made Commandeur de l'Ordre des Arts et des Lettres.

1983

January: *Coast Zone* (Larry Austin/Lancaster and Atlas/direction Atlas) filmed at Synod House, Cathedral of St John the Divine, New York. *Fielding Sixes* (Cage/Lancaster) revived by Ballet Rambert. Fifth City Center season: stage version of *Coast Zone*. Mayor's Award of Honor for Arts and Culture. *Inlets 2* (Cage/Lancaster); *Roaratorio* (Cage/Lancaster). *Inlets 2* also performed by GRCOP, Paris.

1984

Sixth City Center season: *Pictures* (David Behrman/Lancaster). *Cunningham Dance Technique: Elementary Level*, directed by Elliot Caplan, taped at Merce Cunningham Studio. Inducted as Honorary Member of American Academy and Institute of Arts and Letters. *Doubles* (Kosugi/Lancaster), commissioned by American Dance Festival. *Phrases* (Tudor/William Anastasi and Dove Bradshaw). William Anastasi and Dove Bradshaw appointed Artistic Advisers.

1985

Deli Commedia (Pat Richter/Bradshaw) taped with student group, directed by Elliot Caplan, Merce Cunningham Studio. Seventh City Center season: *Native Green* (John King/Anastasi). Choreographic Notations exhibited at Margarete Roeder, New York, together with scores by Cage, Kosugi, Tudor. MacArthur Foundation Fellowship. *Arcade* (Cage/Bradshaw) performed by Pennsylvania Ballet, later by Cunningham Company. Kennedy Center Honors. *Pictures* wins Laurence Olivier Award. *The Dancer and the Dance*, Merce Cunningham in conversation with Jacqueline Lesschaeve (English version), published by Marion Boyars, New York and London.

1986

Eighth City Center season: *Grange EVe* (Kosugi/Anastasi). *Points in Space* (Cage/Anastasi-Bradshaw), directed by Elliot Caplan, taped at BBC Studios, London. Cunningham and Cage receive New York Dance and Performance Award

('Bessie') for lifetime achievement. *Der Tänzer und der Tanz, Gespräche mit Jacqueline Lesschaeve* (German version), published by Fricke Verlag, Frankfurt. *Cunningham Dance Technique: intermediate level*, directed by Elliot Caplan, taped at Merce Cunningham Studio.

1987

Fabrications (Emanuel de Melo Pimenta/Bradshaw). Ninth City Center season: *Shards* (Tudor/Anastasi); revival of *Septet*; stage version of *Points in Space*. SUNY Festival, Merce Cunningham and the New Dance/The Modernist Impulse in Dance, New York. *Carousal* (Kosugi/Bradshaw). Algur H. Meadows Award (Southern Methodist University, Dallas, Texas) for Excellence in the Arts. *Septet* revived by Rambert Dance Company.

1988

Dance/USA National Honor. Repertory season at Joyce Theater, New York: *Eleven* (Robert Ashley/Anastasi). *Five Stone Wind* (Cage-Tudor-Kosugi/Lancaster). *Changing Steps* taped at Sundance Institute, Utah, directed by Elliot Caplan.

1989

Cargo X (Kosugi/Bradshaw); *Field and Figures* (Ivan Tcherepnin/Kristin Jones and Andrew Ginzel). Tenth City Center season. Cunningham receives Légion d'honneur. *August Place* (Michael Pugliese/Africa (Sergei Bougaeul); *Inventions* (Cage/Carl Kielblock). *Septet* revived by Pacific Northwest Ballet.

Jasper Johns in Edisto, South Carolina, 1965

JASPER JOHNS

1930-47

Jasper Johns, born May 15, 1930, in Augusta, Georgia, to William Jasper Johns and Jean Riley Johns. After his parents divorce, he lives with grandparents, W. I. and Montez Johns, in Allendale, South Carolina, and, following the death of his grandfather, with other relatives in several parts of the state. Graduates from high school while living with mother and stepfather in Sumter, South Carolina.

1947-48

Attends the University of South Carolina, in Columbia, for three semesters.

1949-51

Enrols in commercial art school in New York City but quits after two semesters, having been offered a scholarship based on need rather than merit. Works as a messenger boy and shipping clerk until drafted into U.S. Army. Stationed at Fort Jackson, South Carolina, for one year, after which he is sent to Sendai, Japan, for his last six months of service.

1952-54

Having enrolled in Hunter College, he lives on East 83rd Street. He attends classes in the Bronx for one day but does not return. Moving to East 8th Street and Avenue C, works as a clerk in a book store. Introduced to Robert Rauschenberg by Suzi Gablik, he begins in his spare time to help Rauschenberg make objects to be used in window displays. At a party at Sari Dienes' studio, he meets John Cage and Morton Feldman. Sees for the first time Merce Cunningham and Dance Company at the Brooklyn Academy of Music and meets the dancer. He and Rachel Rosenthal move downtown into lofts on Pearl Street, near Rauschenberg's Fulton Street studio. Gives up book store job to devote himself to painting, supporting himself with freelance display work. *Untitled* (Hirshhorn Museum and Sculpture Garden), with cast of Rosenthal's face, *Star* (de Menil Museum) are made at this time. Rauschenberg arranges that *Construction with Toy Piano* (Kunstmuseum Basel) be exhibited in group show at the Tanager Gallery on East 10th Street. Prompted by a dream, he begins first *Flag* painting.

1955

Designs costumes for James Waring's 'Little Kootch Piece', performed at Henry Street Playhouse. Completes *Flag* (The Museum of Modern Art, New York) and, among other works, *Target with Plaster Casts*, *White Flag*, *Tango*, and first paintings of numbers. Upon the death of her father, Rachel Rosenthal moves to California and Rauschenberg rents her studio on Pearl Street.

1956

Paints *Gray Alphabets* and *Canvas*.

1957

Allan Kaprow is responsible for the inclusion of *Green Target* in 'Artists of the New York School, Second Generation' at the Jewish Museum. Having opened his new gallery at 4 East 77th Street, Leo Castelli visits Rauschenberg to look at recent work. When it is mentioned that Johns lives in the loft below, he remembers having seen the painting at the Jewish Museum and expresses a desire to meet the artist. At Johns's studio, Castelli suggests an exhibition. *Flag* is exhibited in 'New Work' at Leo Castelli in May. Continuing to incorporate objects into his work, paints *Book*, *Newspaper*, and *Drawer*.

1958

Castelli holds the first exhibition of Johns's work in January, and Alfred H. Barr acquires *Target with Four Faces*, *Green Target*, and *White Numbers* for The Museum of Modern Art. With Emile de Antonio and Rauschenberg, produces 'The 25-Year Retrospective Concert of the Music of John Cage' at Town Hall. Reading Motherwell's *Dada Painters and Poets* prompts first visit to the Arensberg Collection at the Philadelphia Museum of Art. The Pearl Street building is condemned by the city. Moves into Front Street studio. Makes first sculptures, *Light Bulb I* and *Flashlight*, and *Three Flags* (Whitney Museum of American Art) and *Tennyson* (Des Moines Art Center).

1959

Reads Lebel's *Marcel Duchamp*. Has exhibitions at Galleria d'Arte del Naviglio, Milan, and Galerie Rive Droite, Paris. Dorothy Miller includes nine of his paintings in 'Sixteen Americans' at The Museum of Modern Art. Begins to include the names of colours in his paintings: *False Start*, *Jubilee*, *Out the Window*. Marcel Duchamp visits his studio with critic Nicolas Calas.

1960

Castelli exhibits paintings from the previous year; the Columbia Museum of Art in South Carolina shows work of the last six. Larry Rivers introduces Johns to Tatyana Grosman, Director of Universal Limited Art Editions, Inc. After inviting him to begin lithography, she delivers stones to the Front Street studio. He draws the first image for the portfolio *0-9*, which will not be published until 1963, and *Target*. Paints *Painting with Two Balls* and makes two *Painted Bronze* sculptures, one representing a coffee can filled with brushes and the other two Ballantine Ale cans. With Rauschenberg and de Antonio, produces a concert of Merce Cunningham and Dance Company at the Phoenix Theater on Second Avenue. Spending the summer in Nags Head, North Carolina, he paints the large *Figure 5* (Centre Pompidou, Paris), commissioned by Robert Scull, and the first *0 through 9*, in which the ten figures are superimposed.

1961

Shows drawings, sculpture, and lithographs at Castelli. Buys a house in Edisto Beach, South Carolina, where he paints seven *0 through 9* variations for his exhibition at Galerie Rive Droite. One of the paintings is purchased by the Tate Gallery. With David Tudor, Niki de Saint-Phalle, Rauschenberg, and Jean Tinguely, he participates in a programme at the U.S. Embassy Theater in Paris. His contribution is a large target made of flowers and a painting which announces an *Entr'Acte* that never occurs. In Edisto, paints *Map* (The Museum of Modern Art) and *By the Sea*. On Front Street, he makes a number of paintings in grey, including *Good Time Charley*, *Liar*, *No*, and *Painting Bitten by a Man*.

1962

Continues the grey paintings – *4 the News*, *Fool's House*, *Zone* (Kunsthaus Zürich). Following the large preparatory drawing, paints *Diver*. An exhibition of his work opens Galerie Ileana Sonnabend in Paris.

1963

Moves into penthouse on Riverside Drive, working there and in South Carolina. Exhibits paintings at Castelli. Makes *Numbers* (Philadelphia Museum of Art) in sculpmetal on canvas as an experiment for a much larger work which Philip Johnson has commissioned for the New York State Theater at Lincoln Center. Becomes a founding Director of the Foundation for Contemporary Performance Arts, Inc. George Wittenborn, Inc. publishes *Jasper Johns*, by Leo Steinberg, the first monograph on the artist's work.

1964

Retrospective exhibition opens at the Jewish Museum, New York, and is shown at the Whitechapel Art Gallery, London. *Numbers* is installed for the opening of the New York State Theater. Visits Hawaii with John Cage and Lois Long. Continues to Tokyo, where he paints *Watchman*, *Souvenir*, and *Souvenir 2*. Returning to New York, he paints *According to What*.

1965

Retrospective exhibition opens at Pasadena Art Museum. Awarded prize, VI International Exhibition of Graphic Art, Ljubljana. *Skin with O'Hara Poem*, a collaboration with poet Frank O'Hara, is published by ULAE.

1966

Drawings are exhibited at the National Collection of Fine Arts, Washington, D.C. During his third trip to Japan, fire destroys his Edisto Beach house and studio, as well as numerous works by himself and others.

1967

Contributes illustrations for the title poem to *In Memory of My Feelings*, the book of Frank O'Hara poems published by The Museum of Modern Art shortly after the poet's death. Becomes Artistic Adviser to the Merce Cunningham Dance Company. Moves from Riverside Drive, staying at the Chelsea Hotel until an old Provident Loan Society building on Houston Street can be renovated as studio and residence. During the months needed for this work, he uses David Whitney's loft on Canal Street as a studio. Paints *Map (Based on Buckminster Fuller's Dymaxion Airocean World)*. The 30' × 15' work is shown vertically in the Fuller dome which is the American pavilion at Expo '67 in Montreal. Decides to re-work the painting when he sees the installation. Introduces the flagstone motif in *Harlem Light* and paints *Screen Piece*, the first of five paintings to have the title. Receives a prize at VII International Exhibition of Graphic Art, Ljubljana. Three paintings represent him in IX Bienal de São Paulo, where he is one of ten prize winners.

1968

Begins *Voice 2*. Works for the first time at Gemini G.E.L., Los Angeles, on a series of large *Figure* lithographs. Designs posters for the Merce Cunningham Dance Company and publishes the image as a screen print, *Target with Four Faces*. Supervises the decor for 'Walkaround Time', which is based on Marcel Duchamp's *La Mariée mise à nu par ses célibataires, même*. Executes costumes for this dance and for 'RainForest'.

1969

At Gemini, completes ten *Figure* lithographs. In printing these, several colours of ink are blended on the roller in order to apply them to the printing plate at one time. Also models the reliefs from which moulds are cast for embossing six different images in lead. Designs poster for the Vietnam Moratorium Committee. Makes costumes for Cunningham's 'Canfield'. Receives an Honorary Degree of Doctor of Humane Letters from University of South Carolina. Monograph, *Jasper Johns*, by Max Kozloff, is published by Harry N. Abrams, Inc.

1970

Richard S. Field catalogues 'Jasper Johns: Prints 1960-1970', with an exhibition at the Philadelphia Museum of Art. The Museum of Modern Art, New York, opens 'Jasper Johns: Lithographs', organized by Riva Castleman. Executes costumes for Merce Cunningham's 'Second Hand'. Receives the Creative Arts Awards Citation for Painting from Brandeis University.

1971

Completes his re-working of *Map (Based on Buckminster Fuller's Dymaxion Airocean World)* (Museum Ludwig). The painting is exhibited at The Museum of Modern Art, where Merce Cunningham performs 'Loops' in front of the painting. Finishes *Voice 2* (Kunstmuseum Basel), which he began in 1968, and paints *Decoy*, which derives from a lithograph of the same title and date. The Blackwood Productions film, *Decoy*, follows some of Johns's work on the print. The six *Fragments – According to What* are made at Gemini.

1972

Paints the large *Untitled* (Museum Ludwig) on four panels, incorporating images of walls and body parts and his first use of the cross-hatch motif. Makes first screen print with Hiroshi Kawanishi and Takeshi Shimada of Simca Print Artists. When Vera Lindsay suggests that he illustrates a manuscript version of 'Waiting for Godot', he expresses a preference for unpublished work by Samuel Beckett. Costumes Merce Cunningham's 'TV Rerun' and 'Landrover'. Receives the Skowhegan Medal for Painting from the Skowhegan School for Painting and Sculpture, Maine. Acquires house and studio in the French West Indies.

1973

Designs decor for Merce Cunningham's 'Un Jour ou deux' for the Paris Opera Ballet. In November, visits Samuel Beckett in Paris to discuss the possibility of a collaboration.

Continues graphic work at Simca Print Artists (*Flags I* and *Flags II*) and ULAE (*Decoy II*). Is elected a member of the National Institute of Arts and Letters, New York. Moves to Stony Point, New York.

1974

While in St. Martin, F. W. I., begins to receive Beckett's five English translations from his six 'Foirades'. Paints *Scent* (Bayerische Staatsgemäldesammlungen, Staatsgalerie moderner Kunst, Munich) and *Corpse and Mirror*, the first works based entirely on the cross-hatch motif. At Atelier Crommelynck in Paris, begins etchings and book design for the work with Beckett. Attends opening of 'Jasper Johns Drawings' at the Museum of Modern Art in Oxford. The Arts Council of Great Britain also shows the exhibition in Sheffield, Coventry, Liverpool, Leeds, and London.

1975

Paintings include *The Barber's Tree*, *The Dutch Wives*, and *Weeping Women*. At Gemini, alters plates for grey version of *Four Panels from Untitled 1972*. Continues work with Aldo Crommelynck in Paris. Contributed a print to portfolio of seven prints recording collaborations with Merce Cunningham and Dance Company.

1976

Shows paintings from 1973 to 1975 at Leo Castelli, 4 East 77th Street. This is his last exhibition at this address, where his work has been shown since 1958. The completed book, *Foirades/Fizzles* – five texts by Samuel Beckett, 33 etchings by Johns, protected by a lithograph-lined box – is published by Petersburgh Press.

1977

Receives the Skowhegan Medal for Graphics in April. David Whitney organizes the 'Jasper Johns' retrospective for the Whitney Museum of American Art. From New York it moves to Cologne, Paris, London (Hayward Gallery), Tokyo, and San Francisco.

1978

Paints *Céline* (Kunstmuseum Basel) and *Usuyuki* ('thin snow'). Executes decor for Merce Cunningham's 'Exchange', his last work as Artistic Adviser for the Company.

1979

Continues working with cross-hatch motif and paints the Tantra-influenced *Dancers on a Plane*. Gemini G.E.L. and ULAE publish new lithographs. Christian Geelhaar organizes the exhibition 'Jasper Johns: Working Proofs' for the Kunstmuseum Basel. The exhibition travels to museums in Munich, Frankfurt, Hanover, Copenhagen, Stockholm, Barcelona, Hasselt, and London.

1980

Paints second version of *Dancers on a Plane* (Tate Gallery) and, the first of three, *Tantric Detail*. In February, Katrina Martin completes 'Hanafuda: Jasper Johns', her 16mm film of Johns working with Simca Print Artists in New York. Is elected a foreign member of L'Académie Royale des Beaux Arts in Stockholm.

1981

Tantric Detail II and *Tantric Detail III* are painted, as are the first two large *Between the Clock and the Bed* paintings, one in encaustic and one in oil. 'Jasper Johns: Drawings', at Castelli's 420 West Broadway gallery, contains almost all drawings of 1970-1980. All prints from 1977 to 1981 are exhibited at Thomas Segal Gallery in Boston.

1982

New work includes *In the Studio* and *Perilous Night*, which incorporates an image of John Cage's score. ULAE publishes Judith Goldman's *Jasper Johns: 17 Monotypes* to coincide with the Whitney Museum's exhibition 'Jasper Johns: Savarin Monotypes', which then travels to Dallas, Ljubljana, Basel, Oslo, Stockholm, and London (Tate Gallery).

1983

Paints *Racing Thoughts* (Whitney Museum of American Art), *Ventriloquist* (The Museum of Fine Arts, Houston), and the third *Between the Clock and the Bed* (Virginia Museum of Fine Arts). Makes a group of large ($37\frac{5}{8}'' \times 96\frac{5}{8}''$) monotypes, eight variations of the cross-hatch theme.

1984

Leo Castelli exhibits paintings since 1978 at his Greene Street gallery. Paints a second *Racing Thoughts* in monochrome. *Jasper Johns Drawings 1954-1984*, with text by David Shapiro, is published by Harry N. Abrams, Inc. Richard Francis' *Jasper Johns* is added to the Abbeville Press Modern Masters Series. Elected Fellow, American Academy of Arts and Sciences, Boston.

1985

Summer, the first of 'The Seasons' group, is painted in St. Martin, F. W. I. Makes an etching of the same subject as frontispiece for *Wallace Stevens Poems*, published by The Arion Press.

1986

Designs poster for 'Jasper Johns: A Print Retrospective', which opens at The Museum of Modern Art in May. Organized by Riva Castleman, the exhibition is later shown in eight other museums in Germany, Spain, Austria, the United States, and Japan. 'Jasper Johns: L'Oeuvre Graphique de 1960 à 1985' is exhibited at Fondation Maeght in St. Paul de Vence. Completes *Winter*, *Fall*, *Spring* paintings and numerous related drawings. Receives the Gold Medal for Graphic Art from the American Academy and Institute of Arts and Letters and is awarded the Wolf Prize for Painting from the Wolf Foundation in Israel.

1987

Castelli's 'Jasper Johns: The Seasons' is the first showing of the four paintings and related drawings and prints. Moves from Houston Street studio to mid-town Manhattan. Continues work on copper plates for 'The Seasons' etchings. 'Foirades/Fizzles: Echo and Allusion in the Art of Jasper Johns' opens at Wight Art Gallery, University of California, Los Angeles, and travels to four other cities in the United States.

1988

Under the auspices of the Philadelphia Museum of Art, Mark Rosenthal organizes the exhibition 'Jasper Johns: Work Since 1974' for the American Pavilion of the XLIII Venice Biennale, and Johns is awarded the Grand Prize, the Golden Lion. In October, the same exhibition is shown at the Philadelphia Museum. Completes two prints, experimenting with carborundum, a technique suggested a year or two earlier by Maurice Payne, who prints the editions. Walker Art Center, Minneapolis, acquires from the artist more than 200 prints in various media, establishing the only complete collection of his published graphic work. In 'Jasper Johns, Bruce Nauman, David Salle' at the Castelli Gallery, exhibits four recent works, including *Untitled* (Hirshhorn Museum and Sculpture Garden), containing references to Picasso's *Le Chapeau de paille au feuillage bleu* of 1936. One of these paintings, *The Bath*, is acquired by the Kunstmuseum Basel. Helps organize the 25th Anniversary Exhibition to Benefit the Foundation for Contemporary Performance Arts at Leo Castelli and Brooke Alexander Galleries. Brandeis University awards him the Creative Arts Awards Medal for Painting, and he is inducted into the American Academy of Arts and Letters.

ACKNOWLEDGEMENTS

Our special thanks go to Jasper Johns, Mimi Johnson and David Vaughan for their painstaking research on the three chronologies. We are extremely grateful to Mark Lancaster, Edvard Lieber, Matthew Marks and Ajit Mookerjee for their invaluable help and advice. We should also like to thank: Michael Bloom, Kathan Brown and the staff of Crown Point Press, Elliot Caplan, Leo Castelli, Douglas Druick, Hayden Hopkins, Charles Mabey and the staff of BAS Printers, James Klosty, Uwe Kraus and the staff of Dr. Cantz'sche Druckerei, Michael Meagher, Jim Meyer, Susan Ralston, Simon Rendall, Margarete Roeder, Michael Stier, Robert Violette and Andrew Wylie. We are grateful to the Cunningham Dance Foundation for permission to reprint excerpts from their catalogue of film and video.

Photographic credits: Charles Atlas p. 77; Rudolph Burckhardt pp. 116, 118, 126 and 128; Prudence Cuming Associates pp. 36-45; p. 146, courtesy Cunningham Dance Foundation; Bevan Davies p. 93; Timothy Greenfield-Sanders pp. 4, 35, 55 and 91; Clemens Kalischer p. 59; James Klosty pp. 65, 68-69, 70-71, 73, 74-75 and 156; Barbara Morgan p. 57; Ugo Mulas p. 160; Eric Pollitzer pp. 122 and 123; Richard Rutledge pp. 62, 63 and 67; Martin Silver pp. 60-61; Glenn Steigelman pp. 97, 105, 107, 109-10 and 113; Terry Stevenson p. 79; Jim Strong pp. 94, 95, 100 and 102; Dorothy Zeidman pp. 92, 96 and 99; Zindman/Fremont p. 101.